THE THIRD CURVE

THE
THIRD
CURVE

The End of Growth
as we know it

Mansoor Khan

Deal with Reality
or
Reality will deal with you.

- Unknown

THE THIRD CURVE: The End of Growth as we know it

First edition 2013

ISBN-13: 978-81-926351-0-1

10 9 8 7 6 5 4 3 2 1

Typeset in Arno Pro and Museo

Designed and typeset by Anand Prahlad

Illustrated by Sahil Shah

Printed in India at TRIKKON, Lower Parel, Mumbai

❄

Contents

Acknowledgements

My initial journey with this book started in the year 2001 with my growing interest in Peak Oil. The more I researched the subject, the more clearly did I see the co-relation between this predicament and its impacts on the world economy and on our day-to-day lives. In fact, those who studied Peak Oil were anticipating and predicting the Economic Collapse which, when it finally occurred, in 2008, spread like an epidemic across continents, confusing the very powers entrusted with our well-being. It was amazing that no one was talking about the real cause of the crisis, which was undoubtedly energy related.

At the end of ten years, my research had crystallised into a body of knowledge worthy of being tested in select academic and intellectual circles. Around the same time, I was invited to various institutions of repute to make a presentation on what was, apparently, a pressing relevant subject. Institutions like The Energy & Resources Institute (TERI), New Delhi; Indian Institute of Management (IIM), Bangalore; and The Indian School of Business (ISB), Hyderabad. The strong responses convinced me that the time was, indeed, ripe for a book. And as I started working on it, piecing the jigsaw and fleshing out the logic, the book drew its own supporters and benefactors. Here are the people, who with their enthusiasm, conviction, and support, made this project a working delight.

My strongest supporters from the outset were, of course, my ever-loving family members - my wife Tina, my daughter Zayn, and my son Pablo - who listened patiently to my ideas and theories at various stages of their evolution. Tina gave me the latitude to explore a space that made this journey possible, for which I am truly and exceptionally grateful. It was her patience and understanding that gave me strength to explore and hold onto a perspective that rose against the grain of popular belief.

My thanks to Murzban Shroff, a close friend and himself a writer of repute, of the much-acclaimed book *Breathless in Bombay*. Murzban related so closely to the subject matter that he took it onto himself to get involved in every aspect – from the narrative edit, to styles of illustration, to the cover design and book layout – in order to ensure that the book did not lack anything and that it would deliver its message as strongly and clearly as possible. Murzban also provided me moral support on a daily basis to get through the daunting task of publishing this book.

My thanks to the book designer, Anand Prahlad, for taking up the challenge of creating a theoretically radical yet visually appealing book. Anand, with his cool temperament and balanced approach, was ever-willing to accommodate the evolutionary changes that the book went through.

My thanks to Sahil Shah for defining the unique style of sketches that illustrate this book. With his own brand of rebellion and artistic humour, Sahil has lightened the harsh realities of the subject matter.

A very special thanks to my friend Montosh Lal with whom I share a lot of common ideologies. Montosh selflessly gave his artistic inputs and brought to the book his long years of design experience.

Special thanks to my friend Aline Ranc who surprised me with her first-class line-editing skills. Aline understands the issues in the book so well that she also contributed significantly to the creative edit.

I thank Mita Kapur of Siyahi, a literary consultancy, for her generous help and support in helping me navigate the maze that is publishing.

My warm thanks to my friend Nita Bali, who being cued into the subject of Peak Oil herself, gave my early drafts the first vital thumbs-up.

Navin Muralidharan, a friend who I initiated into the subject of Peak Oil, became so convinced about this reality that he keeps me updated on a daily basis with news of the unravelling effects of energy decline on the financial world. I thank Navin for providing regular, real-world verification of the subject matter of this book.

Thanks also to my resourceful friend Shumita Didi for expediting the process of obtaining ISBN numbers.

My warmest thanks to my aunt, Dr Najma Heptulla (Ex-deputy Chairperson, Rajya Sabha), for taking my objectives as her own and helping to create the right support systems for the book.

My collective thanks to the innumerable friends, acquaintances and visitors to my farm, who listened with an open mind to my impassioned views, sometimes shocked and shaken by the facts but always receptive to the truth. Their individual response was, indeed, the perfect testing ground for each round of improvement that the book went through.

And finally, my thanks to you, dear reader, who made the tough choice to pick up this book despite its sombre title: *The Third Curve – The End of Growth as we know it.*

Introduction

"Growth plummets".
"Core sector growth rate dips to 5.7%".
"Finance minister announces stimulus package to boost growth".

The Modern World is obsessed with growth. We worship growth. Growth is our religion.

Daily, we hear thousands of statements about this phenomenon called "growth". We are now conditioned to believe that growth is a natural reaction of a society and culture that is restlessly striving to improve, develop, progress and outdo itself.

Yet we fail to clarify that we don't mean any old kind of growth. We don't mean cyclical, limited biological growth that entities like plants, animals, humans and just about everything in nature follows. They all grow for a while and then stop growing.

We also do not mean the kind of qualitative growth that makes us love our family, friends, village, town and community increasingly with time.

Firstly, we reduced the notion of growth to a quantitative state. As if that were not enough, we expect it to increase exponentially on a perpetual basis. That is best called **Perpetual Exponential Quantitative Growth.** A mouthful, so best shortened to **PEQG**.

In fact our economic system demands Perpetual Exponential Quantitative Growth (PEQG), which makes an amazingly unreasonable assumption that we have limitless resources on a finite planet. The stunning benefits so far bestowed on industrial man crystallized the myth in classical economics that PEQG is a universal law, a God-given right, and that it can and must be sustained at all costs. This assumption appeared to hold true for the last 150 years as there were vast corners of our planet we had not plundered for resources yet. But that was the first half of the story of the Modern Industrial World.

Now we are in the second half of the story where we have roughly used up half of most of the world's resources that are crucial to running an industrial world. And the key resource that is half gone is **Oil**. Oil is the blood of our industrial world in more ways than people realize. This half-way point of oil depletion is in truth a turning point in modern history – it is called **Peak Oil** and forms the body of this book.

This book illustrates our predicament by contrasting 2 curves. One is an exponential curve of our expectations – the economic paradigm of **Perpetual Exponential Quantitative Growth** (PEQG). And the other is a bell curve that in reality all resources follow and is an introduction to the basic principles of Peak Oil. Through these 2 curves, I will illustrate that in a PEQG paradigm you only have to reach the half-way point (not the end) of oil reserves to be in real trouble. That is to say, when oil has reached the point at which we are drawing the maximum oil (Peak) from the ground. We are at Peak Oil right now.

This is such a landmark moment in industrial history, yet surprisingly few people are aware of it. Now, within years, we start descending the oil curve. From here on, the slope goes only downwards and we can only get less and less oil from the ground. This inverts all the rules of economics! It actually spells the End of Growth. Growth: the very bedrock of modern economics. And that spells financial catastrophe.

If we look at this honestly, we realize that the future that was promised to us in the '50s, '60s and '70s no longer looks possible. Yet we follow the paradigm of Exponential Growth full throttle and reduce all chances of finding a viable solution. This mad quest for Exponential Growth takes a simultaneous toll on the natural fabric of the world as we rape the planet off every and anything that remotely looks like a resource to fuel the ever-rising, blazing inferno that we proudly call our Modern Economic System.

So what is the "solution", people ask?

Easy you might say. The solutions are obvious, right?

Find more oil!

Switch to alternative energies!

Increase energy efficiency!

Develop new technologies, new ways!

That is exactly what this book questions. It examines whether these solutions are indeed solutions or half-truths. Whether alternatives can indeed replace oil. Whether technologies can indeed save us in the face of resource depletion. Whether growth itself can be sustained on a perpetual basis.

It must be understood that this book is not about morality, justice, equity, and environmental consciousness.

It is simply about what is possible and what is not.

It is not about what we should not do.

It is about what we will NOT BE ABLE to do no matter how hard we try.

It is about limits set by the universe.

Namely the Third Curve.

Prelude: 3 phases of Modern Times

Let us review the state of the world as it has evolved since the discovery of oil.

PARADISE TIMES (Till '60s): The Sky is the Limit

Till the '60s we felt the sky was the limit. The horse cart gave way to the motor car. Air travel replaced sea travel. Machines replaced man. And man was free to dream and create even more.

Then on July 20, 1969, man landed on the moon. Breaking the bounds of our little planet appeared to send ripples of boundless expectations for the future. Now anything was possible: we would get unlimited food, eradicate all diseases, live longer, be served by robots, holiday on the Moon or even on Mars. We would soon fly around our cities instead of driving on the road as if contact with good old Mother Earth appeared a bit lowly.

Breaking the bounds of Mother Earth assured us that we were entitled to break all limits of time, space, productivity, comfort. These were **Paradise Times** and the Sky was the Limit.

ECOLOGICAL BREAKDOWN

But as time panned out, we discovered that the future did not look as we had been promised. Starting with the disappearance of the whale, we woke up to species extinction, forest depletion, population explosion, top-soil erosion, ground water depletion, chemicals in our food, cancer, chemicals in everything, more cancer, melting glaciers, dying rivers and finally the big one – Global Warming!

All this we termed and recognized as **Ecological Collapse**. But why was it happening?

We were soon to discover that this was only the beginning of our problems.

FINANCIAL COLLAPSE

So we raced on down the highway of Economic Growth in a way hoping that this would help us offset the ecological crisis by allotting huge funds through well-intentioned organizations to "save" the environment. But then surprisingly, even the structured and controlled human domain of the Financial World started going awry. And each day we woke up to newer realities: rising taxes, rising energy prices, rising food prices, skyrocketing real estate prices, greater inequity, more wars and unrest, and inflated financial bubbles that burst at regular intervals, until we reached 2008 – the year of the Global Economic Collapse.

The subsequent rumblings are muted but there is no cure in sight. Despite the unimaginable quantum of public money to douse the fire, we seem to be in a state of chronic **Financial Collapse**.

And suddenly – the Future ain't what it used to be.

Could all these events be deeply connected in a way that we have not considered before?

I believe they are not paradoxical but inevitably and intimately connected.

Let me show you how.

Part I

2 Curves - Concept vs. Reality

The Mismatch between Money & Resources

Mind vs. Body

I am going to make a rather slow and simplistic beginning to our journey of exploring the way in which we define Money Growth, the phenomenon of Peak Oil and the reasons for Financial Collapse. This is necessary as we need to revisit a lot of basic principles that we take for granted. Only by tracing that path, can we begin to understand the non-negotiable predicament that we, in the modern industrial world, find ourselves in.

So we start at a time far in the past of civilization. That is when a certain **Concept** took root in our minds and we have built upon that **Concept** ever since, to the point that it literally took over every aspect of our **Reality**. It is the concept of Money and the idea that Money must grow with time.

But before we get to that, let us look at how **Concept** and **Reality** interact in general.

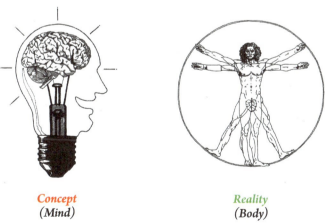

Concept
(Mind)

Reality
(Body)

Our mind comes up with a **Concept**. But to execute it in **Reality** we have to put our body to use.

For instance, our mind comes up with the concept to lift up a glass of water. And our body can move a hand to do it. The **Concept** can be fulfilled by **Reality**.

Next, our mind may suggest that we lift a chair. And our body can lift that chair too. Again **Reality** can match the **Concept**.

But what if our mind came up with the concept of lifting a school bus – with just our body of course? The Body can try but it will not be able to do it. The **Concept** has failed.

In short, the Mind can come up with any concept but it is not necessary that the Body could or even should fulfil that in reality. There are limits to bodies but maybe not to minds. Respecting limits is something that Civilization has collectively baulked at in a peculiar celebration of the symbolic over the real.

Concept vs. Reality

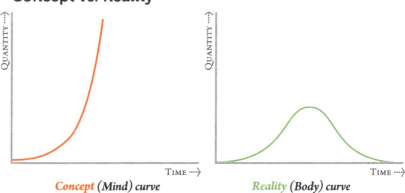

Concept (Mind) curve   *Reality (Body) curve*

SHAPE OF CONCEPT VS. REALITY

Let us say our mind comes up with a **Concept** of the growth of a given quantity that is increasing in a manner that looks like the graph on the left. As you can see, the quantity increases slowly at first but then increases faster and faster with each step. And this goes up forever. This type of growth, which becomes increasingly faster with passing time, is mathematically called **Exponential Growth**. I have deliberately chosen this curve as it represents the behavior of one of the most important concepts in our Modern Industrial World, namely money.

The **Concept** is sky-reaching – INFINITE.

The right graph is the shape of **Reality**. It is a measure of how much the Body is able to deliver to make that **Concept** happen, because remember: our mind can come up with any Concept but the Body eventually has to deliver. This curve starts at zero, goes up sharply to reach a peak and then decays to zero. This shape is called a Bell Curve.

Once again this curve is not arbitrary, as we will see shortly, and it represents the shape of a lot of things in Reality, especially Oil.

So **Reality** is bounded and FINITE.

In other words, the left curve is what the **Concept** **expects,** which is infinite. And the right curve is how much the Body **can give**, in **Reality**, which is finite.

Now you can clearly see that the Body is behaving differently from the Mind and may not be able to give what the **Concept** expects. And that is going to create serious problems of expectations. That is exactly what we are interested in examining.

15

The Mismatch between Concept & Reality

Let us move the 2 curves onto one graph so that we can compare their shapes more closely.

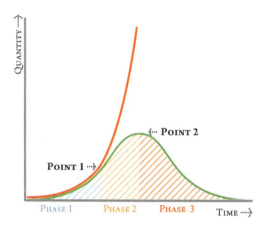

Though there is an obvious mismatch between our **Concept** and **Reality**, it is interesting and important to understand there are similarities too at certain times.

Phase 1 – Paradise Times

In this phase, up to point 1, the **Reality Curve** moves parallel to the **Concept Curve**. This means it does behave like an exponential curve and keeps pace with the **Concept**.

This means that **Reality** in this phase is able to live up to the expectations of the **Concept**.

The Growth of the quantity is TRUE. No wonder we are all happy and we call it **Paradise Times.**

Phase 2 – Body Withers

Beyond point 1 and up to point 2, the **Reality Curve** **stops** behaving like an exponential curve and is not able to keep pace with the **Concept Curve**. Look at the right graph and you can see **Reality** tapering off and slowing down.

The **Concept** can be said to be showing some signs of failure in **Reality**.

The Growth of the quantity is therefore FALSE.

We will see later that this failure results in a withering of the Body that was trying to live up to the **Concept**.

PHASE 3 – Concept Withers

Beyond point 2, the **Reality** Curve in fact goes in a totally opposite direction to the **Concept Curve** and returns to zero.

In other words, whatever your **Concept** was, it has TOTALLY failed!

Growth is IMPOSSIBLE.

We will see later that this failure results in the inversion of the very **Concept** itself. So growth in fact becomes shrinkage.

To understand this in real terms, it is time to draw an analogy with an example of a **Concept** and a **Reality** that you can relate to.

The Coach and the Runner

Coach *Concept*
(Mind)

Runner *Reality*
(Body)

Let us examine the relationship between **Concept** (Mind) and **Reality** (Body) through the example of a Coach and a Runner.

This example is selected to highlight the hazards of exponential thinking especially in the context of the finiteness of performance of a human body. The coach expects results based on a purely mathematical model, while the runner is enticed by the stunning though unreal prospects of performance. Following this example will help us understand how a **Concept Curve** and **Reality Curve** evolve and then interact.

The Coach has a Concept which he claims can make you, the Runner, run at the speed of sound in just 18 months.

"How is that possible?", you wonder.

He explains, "Can you run at 10 km/h?"

"Yes, of course, that is slightly faster than walking".

"After one week, can you run 7% faster at **10.7** km/h?"

"Sure!"

"After one more week, can you run 7% faster at **11.45** km/h?"

"Sure!"

"And after 3 weeks, can you run 7% faster at **12.25** km/h?"

"Sure!"

"Well, that is my Super Concept. Every week you run 7% faster than your speed of the earlier week – nothing more, nothing less. And in 18 months you will break the speed of sound".

SUPER SPEED CHART	
Week #	Speed (kmph)
1	10.7
2	11.45
3	12.25
4	13.11
5	14.03
6	15.01
7	16.06
8	17.18
9	18.38
10	19.67

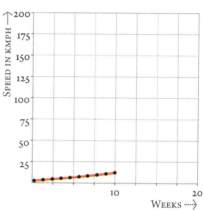

You look at the chart, but after 10 whole weeks, your speed has reached only about 20 km/h from 10 km/h. Hardly a "Super Speed Chart". Besides, the speed of sound is 1,225 km/h. That is 1,000 km/h more. "How can I reach the speed of sound?", you ask.

He gives a cocky smirk and says, "But just see what happens every 10 weeks after that". You notice something amazing. Your speed is doubling every 10 weeks as in the chart below:

SUPER SPEED CHART	
Week #	Speed (kmph)
10	19
20	38
30	76
40	149
50	294
60	579
70	1139

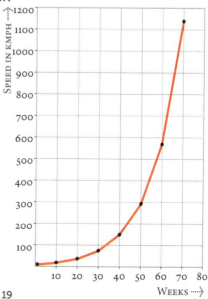

See how it shoots up after the 10th week. Moving faster and faster to the sky.

It suddenly dawns on you how it works. What the Coach has just described is an exponential curve. When the Super Coach is making you run 7% faster than your new speed, it means that your speed is compounding. It is increasing by a greater amount each week. This means your speed is increasing **exponentially**. This means it doubles every 10 weeks!

Indeed, compounding is a **Super Concept**. And that is how in just one and a half years, if you keep up the exponential trend, you will be running at the speed of sound and more!!!

No wonder you agree to his training. BUT, wait a minute! What will be the fees? And he says, "NOTHING".

How come? "Because", the Super Coach says, "I am going to recover that from the sponsors who I have sold this Super Concept to. In fact, I will pay you some money out of the sponsorships. Howzat?"!

Too good to be true and you hop onto his Super Coaching Program.

The Coach and the Runner
PHASE 1 – Paradise Times

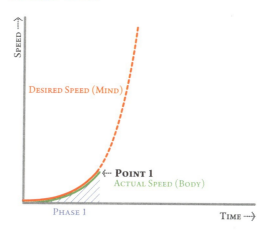

In the first week, he makes you run at **10** km/h as planned. That is just slightly faster than walking!

Then at the end of the first week, he wants you to run 7% faster at **10.7** km/h. And of course you can do that. It is only a small increase.

Then at the end of the second week, you are running 7% faster of **10.7** km/h and that is **11.45** km/h. And so on, as per his Super Chart.

So for 10 weeks you are able to keep up with his set speed and at the end of the 10th week you have almost doubled your speed from **10** km/h to **19.67** km/h. You don't feel any stress. Your body is able to cope with this exponential trend of increasing your speed.

And therefore, because your body is able to cope with the **Concept**, all is well. Your Coach is happy and your Sponsors are thrilled and paying you large amounts of money for your achievements.

These are **Paradise Times**. You are eagerly waiting to hit the speed of sound.

Phase 1
Paradise times

The Coach and the Runner
PHASE 2 – Body Collapse

Coach *Concept*
(Mind)

Runner *Reality*
(Body)

Starting Phase 2 the following week, you notice that you could only increase your speed by 6 % and not the 7% that your coach expects.

The coach will have none of this and he pushes you harder the next week to make up for the lost performance.

But in the next week, your body can only improve your speed by say 4.5% as opposed to 7 %.

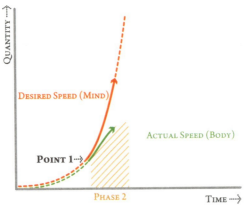

Super Coach does not tell the sponsors about the difference between REALITY and CONCEPT and so the SPONSORS keep looking at his Super Chart posted in their offices and blindly continue betting on you with higher stakes.

Super Coach pushes you harder still and yet your body does only 2.8% better in the 15th week.

You start feeling mentally stressed and focus strictly on training, avoid social contact and secretly start taking steroids to artificially boost your performance in an attempt to match your coach's expectations.

The coach intensifies his training each week and you increase your steroid dosage but the speed percentage only decreases. Your body begins to show obvious signs of breakdown. The more your coach reproaches with structured torture, the more you push, the more your body withers.

The next week, there is only a mere 1.5% increase in speed. Horror of horrors! In fact, your rate of improvement itself is slowing down from 7% to 6% to 4.5% to 2.8% to 1.5%. In other words, you are getting faster… but at a decreasing pace! Unseen to you, your body is crumbling now at a catastrophic pace because of the added mental and physical stress, and of course, the steroids.

Yet all this while, the coach keeps the sponsors blissfully unaware of your real performance and they are busy selling tickets to your Super Show of breaking the speed of sound. They are only aware of your performance for the first 12 weeks and that has convinced them that this is how the trend is going to be forever. So everyone's perceived financial gains continue skywards as per the left curve of Concept but your performance is tapering off as per the right curve of the Reality of your body.

And now you reach the end of **Phase 2** – the top of the **Reality Curve**. You clock 0% increase that week!

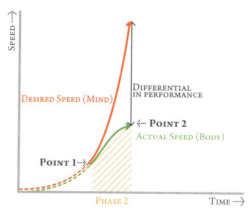

You are running the fastest you ever have but with a body propped up with steroids and no increase in speed.

The **Reality** cannot be concealed any further. Your SPONSORS hit the ceiling as they discover that your COACH has not been sharing the reality – the slowdown of your improvement. In a messy showdown your sponsors withdraw.

This is a double whammy. On the one hand your body is a wreck. On the other hand the huge amounts of money the sponsors have already paid are a write off. Any possible future gains evaporate and your financial world comes crashing down.

You realize that you are collapsing both from the outside and from within. In Mind and Body. In Health and in Wealth. In **Concept** and in **Reality**.

24

The Coach and the Runner
PHASE 3 – Concept Collapse

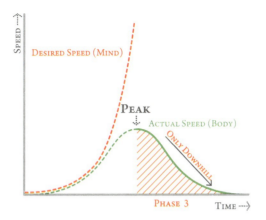

You are at the peak of your performance, at the top of the Reality/Body Curve. From now on, it will obviously be downhill, because the more stress and steroids you take, results, in fact, in a decrease of your performance. Because that is how the Body behaves. Clearly you are in a crisis.

You have to make a choice.

How the future pans out in **Phase 3** depends on what changes you make in your paradigm and the choices you make. But if you were to ask me, this is what I would say.

You must do 2 things at this point in time.

1. Kill the Concept.
Namely sack your Super Coach and abandon his crazy concept of eternally increasing your speed exponentially because that is just his Mind insisting on an infinite Concept.

2. Save your Body.
Stop taking the steroids immediately, or you will die prematurely because you have to deal with the limits of your Body.

Or would you rather have it the other way around: Save the Concept and Kill your Body?

I know what I would do, but then again, the choice is yours. It is your body.

Phase 3
Concept Collapse

BUT what if this example did not apply only to *your* body? What if it applied to all of us collectively on this planet? Even more, what if it applied to the whole Earth and everything on it?

I am sure the choice would have to be different.

To examine this, it is time to go back to the **Concept** and **Reality** that I really wanted to talk about.

The Actual Concept & Reality

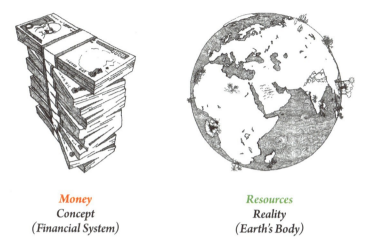

Money
Concept
(Financial System)

Resources
Reality
(Earth's Body)

After the analogy of the Coach and the Runner, we come to the Actual **Concept** and **Reality** that this book is about.

This time the **Concept** is **Money**.

And **Reality** is all known **Resources** on our planet.

This time the Mind is the **Financial System** and the Body is that of **Mother Earth**.

This time we let the Mind of the Financial System come up with a **Concept** and we will take everything from the Body of Mother Earth to fulfill it.

That **Concept** is money and money must grow.

Then why did I give the example of the Coach and the Runner if we were going to talk about Money and the Earth?

To understand this, we have to first change our perception of the Earth significantly from what our industrial mindset has engrained in us. The Earth is not a huge, inanimate hunk of mud, rock, ores, minerals, etc. that can spew out resources at whatever rate we wish for human purpose alone. It is not to be viewed as a storehouse of resources for us to extract, loot and dispose of. That is the classical, rigid and narrow viewpoint of a culture called Industrial Civilization. The same culture that revels in being the most advanced but finds itself mired in a domino effect of crises.

The Earth in fact is a complex organism. It is as living as each of us. We are merely a part of it like everything else on it. Everything is intimately connected to make the whole organism work. The Earth in fact is a body just like our runner. It is living.

This was no great news to the primitive and indigenous people who have walked gently on the Earth for tens and hundreds of thousands of years before civilized man appeared on the scene. The Red Indians, the Pygmies, the Yanomamo, the Eskimo, the Adivasi and innumerable other indigenous cultures all the way back to hunter/gatherers, derisively called primitive, always perceived every part of the Earth as a single living whole – the rivers, the clouds, the wind, the rain, the soil and even the rocks and mountains. And that is the reason why they treated it with humility, reverence and a sense of gratefulness. This, in turn preserved the Earth for so long in its awesome grandeur and beauty – the original and true Garden of Eden.

Then came along a totally different kind of culture called Civilization. This culture proved to be diametrically opposite to all others before it. With its peculiar worldview of ownership, Civilization, starting with agriculture (last 10,000 years) and then building up to the Modern Industrial Civilization (last 150 years), has efficiently destroyed much of the living planet in an ecological blink of the eye. It treated the Earth, our mother organism, as a one-time, exploitable and disposable source of goodies that are needed to run our financial system, meaning to make money grow.

With money growth as our ultimate objective we take all kinds of health capital from the Earth and pass it through our single-minded and destructive industrial system to convert it into financial capital. That is the sole purpose of the Modern Industrial World.

It is only when we perceive the Earth as a single living organism that we get a new insight into the stresses we are putting on the Earth's Body by our habits and insistences. And this perspective automatically defines LIMITS – something that modern economics does not believe in.

In the same way that everything needed to achieve the Super Coach's Concept for the Runner came from the Runners body, everything that has to make the Financial System work has to come from the Earth's Body. And all bodies are limited. Yet Modern Economics, much like the Super Coach, does not believe in limits.

Let us delve further into the impacts of this brutal version of **Concept** and **Reality**.

The Actual Concept
MONEY CURVE (Mind) – Laws of Economics

At some point in the history of Civilization, man came up with the **Concept** of money, making it a symbolic token to represent the value of goods and services, facilitating trade.

This apparently innocuous creation of the mind inadvertently spawned a chain of **Concepts** that defined how money must behave.

So let us trace the evolution of these **Concepts**.

Concept 1: Money is a TRUE representation of value of a good or service.

> **Reason:** Maybe… maybe not. But it certainly makes trade easier so we accepted this rule.

Concept 2: Money must GROW with time by a factor of P%.

> **Reason:** This concept again did not intrinsically originate out of greed, but out of a natural desire to be productive. For instance, a hard-working person sees a lazy person doing nothing with his money. So he tells the lazy person: "If you don't do something productive with your money then I can". Quickly and naturally, the idea of enterprising people taking a loan from lazy people, then producing goods or services (usually through hard work) and then earning profits, became common place. The lazy person was happy to be an onlooker to his money earning a component of the profit called interest. The mutual benefit of lender and borrower facilitated this rule to be embodied and useful goods to be made.
>
> In time, this consolidated into the non-negotiable law of the Time-Value of Money.

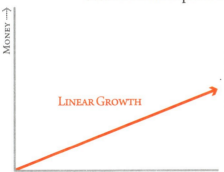

So Money MUST grow. The Growth is linear. It goes up in a straight line.

Concept 3 : Growth of money must COMPOUND and grow faster and faster with time.

> **Reason:** This is the tricky one! This was nothing but a recursion of Concept 2. The logical mind could not have avoided this application of a concept to a concept. Add the earned interest to the capital. Earn interest on the interest. Ad infinitum! Compounding makes money increase exponentially. Faster and faster with each step.
>
> So naturally, the compounding of money was applauded as an inherent beauty of **Concepts**.

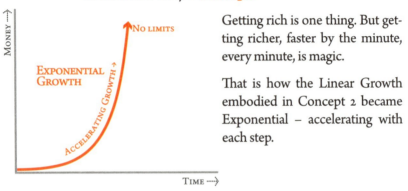

Getting rich is one thing. But getting richer, faster by the minute, every minute, is magic.

That is how the Linear Growth embodied in Concept 2 became Exponential – accelerating with each step.

Concept 4: Compounding growth must be PERPETUAL – go on forever and ever and ever.

> **Reason:** Well, why not? Such an elegantly profitable concept MUST always hold true.

And so, the bold and audacious **Money Curve** was defined as an **Exponential**.

Now you know why we selected the Exponential Curve as the **Concept Curve**.

By definition, money starts growing slowly, yet increases its speed by turning its nose closer to the vertical with each step.

Faster and faster is the climb. Sky-bound. Without limits. Forever. Or so the idea goes.

That is why I illustrated the same through a Runner and his Coach. The Coach had a similar exponential scheme. You will see as we go along, there is a lot in common between the Coach-Runner analogy and the reality of our economic model.

Money must follow **Perpetual Exponential Quantitative Growth**. I call it **PEQG** for short.

Most people simply call it Growth but that is as misleading as calling a nuclear bomb a large firecracker.

PEQG is a monster, overruling all other laws.

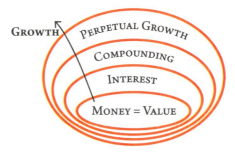

That monster, cleverly wrapped in layers of concepts, happens to be the founding principle of **Modern Economics**.

And Modern Economics, my dear readers, is the very bedrock of the belief of Modern Industrial Civilization.

Why do we love this monster called PEQG?

Just like the runner was lured by a crazy concept with dreams of achieving unbelievable speeds, so also are we drawn by the obsession for limitless growth in our economic model. Because it is not just growth we are talking about. It is **Perpetual Exponential Quantitative Growth (PEQG)**. And this monster promises to make you unbelievably rich… very often without doing anything.

Let us say you put Rs. 10 lakhs in a fixed deposit that gives 7% compound interest and then just wait. It doubles in 10 years. So at the end of a decade you have 20 lakhs.

And then, in another decade the 20 lakhs doubles to become 40 lakhs. And so on…

In just 10 decades, a century later, your capital of 10 lakhs becomes more than **100 crores!**

MONEY GROWTH CHART	
Year #	MONEY (in Lakhs)
10	20
20	40
30	80
40	160
50	320
60	640
70	1,280
80	2,560
90	5,120
100	10,240

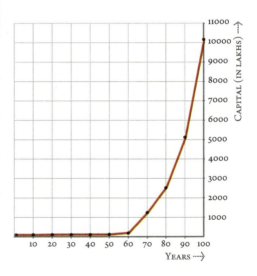

That is 1024 times the original capital in 100 years!

Now who would not want that?

BUT

**The more we produce, the more we use.
And one of the prime components to perpetuate growth in an
Industrial World is Energy.**

Take a look at the graph below that shows the direct correlation between money growth and energy consumption over the last 150 years. So if money has to grow 1024 times then we also use 1024 times the energy, which is mainly fossil fuels: Coal, Oil and Natural Gas.

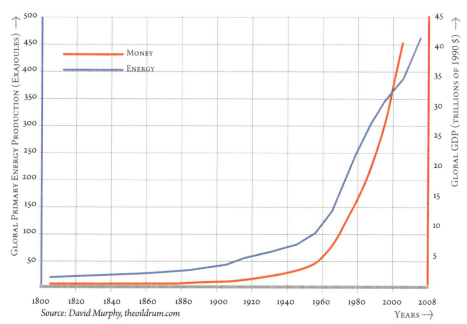

Source: David Murphy, theoildrum.com

And where do the inputs that drive this **Money Concept** come from?

They come from the BODY. The body of the Earth.

And can the body of the Earth give us all this in the exponential quantities that we demand? Forever?

To examine that, it is time to move back to the **Reality Curve**.

Actual Reality
RESOURCE CURVE (Body) – Laws of Geology

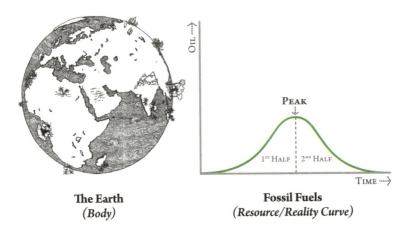

The Earth
(Body)

Fossil Fuels
(Resource/Reality Curve)

The reality of the Modern Industrial World is energy. And 86% of the energy that runs it comes from Fossil Fuels – Coal, Natural Gas and Oil. So Fossil Fuels are the most important component of our natural capital.

The future of Financial Growth (as shown on the graph on previous page), is directly dependent on total energy availability. And fossil fuels run the world. And among fossil fuels, **Oil** is our key industrial energy source. A point that is amply explained in Chapter 2 of this book.

This section is crucial to our understanding of the pattern of resource availability. It is ironic that no aspect of our education system makes us aware that the **Resource Curve** is governed by the geology of our planet. With passing time the Earth gives us most of its resources in a BELL SHAPED curve. Ironically, the peak of the bell curve is also the half-way point of depletion of any resource. In the case of oil, the peak is when we have extracted only half the oil from that well. From there, you can only get less.

The Earth DOES NOT give us resources at a steady pace from the beginning to the end. The extraction rate of natural resources such as iron, copper, minerals, water, coal, natural gas, oil and innumerable others obeys the BELL CURVE.

Nor can we simply put a larger pump and change the pace of extraction to suit our will.

This is the reason why I selected the BELL CURVE for the **Reality Curve**.

This is the single most vital gap in our understanding of our energy predicament. These wrong perceptions arise because we think of the Earth as a tank or a storehouse and so we imagine it will behave like one. This is simply not true for the Earth.

No matter what you do, the Earth gives any resource in the shape of a BELL CURVE. And that has serious limitations on our **Concept Curve** as we will see in greater detail in the rest of this book.

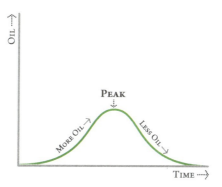

For now, let us understand that if we want our Exponential **Concept Curve** of Money to work, we have to be worried about the Bell **Reality Curve** of Resources because it is the shape of this body curve that dictates the upper limits of what is possible. This is much like the body of the Runner put an upper limit on how far the **Concept** of the Super Coach could be achieved. And as you can see, the 2 curves look shockingly different.

Let us examine how the real world versions of **Concept** and **Reality** behave and interact.

MONEY GROWTH (CONCEPT) VS OIL PRODUCTION (REALITY)

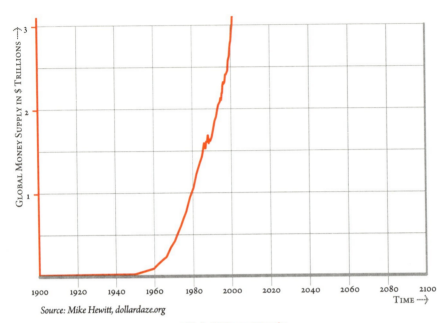

Source: Mike Hewitt, dollardaze.org

Global Money Supply

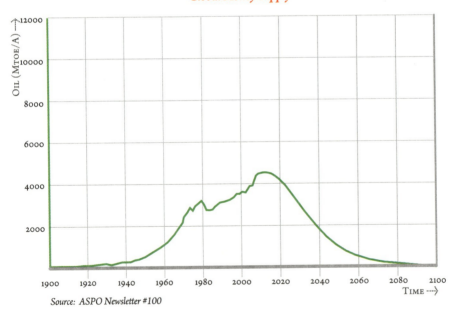

Source: ASPO Newsletter #100

Global Oil Production

Real World Versions of Concept and Reality

In the real world, our **Concept** is **Money Growth**.

And the **Reality** that makes that possible is **Oil Production**.

The upper graph (opposite page) shows actual figures of the **Global Money Supply** by year. You can see it has shaped as an exponential curve, just like we said our Money Curve should behave.

The lower graph is the **Global Oil Production** by year. It has followed a bell curve, or the theoretical Reality Curve, while trying to fulfill the

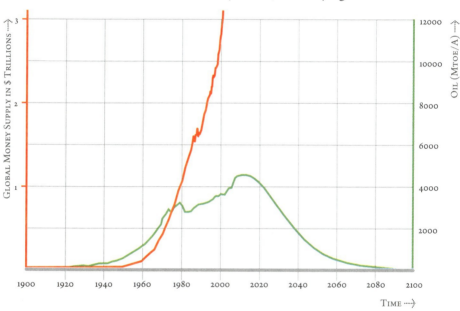

top curve of exponential economic expectation. I remind the reader that I have chosen Global Oil Production as the Reality Curve because Oil is the defining factor for Industrial Growth and therefore Money Growth, a fact that we will explore in detail in Chapter 2.

To see how they interact, let's put them together (as shown above). We can clearly see that we are getting the same 3 phases in time as had happened with the Runner and Coach. Let us examine them one by one.

PHASE 1 – Paradise Times

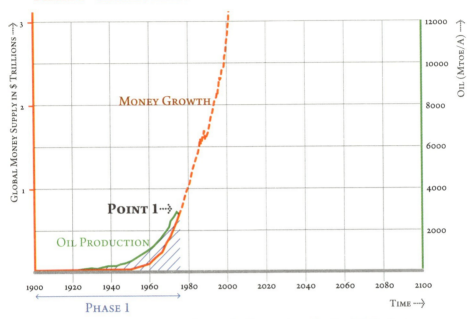

Starting **Phase 1**, we can see that in the beginning, the Earth's Body, just like the Runner's body, was able to keep pace with exponential demands. We were able to draw Oil (and other fossil fuels) from the Earth in an exponential pattern. It is possible, as we mentioned earlier, because this is the only part where the **Reality Curve** increases more or less exponentially and is able to keep pace with the **Concept Curve**, which is always exponential. Notice how the Money and Oil curve in the graph above are running fairly parallel in this phase.

Because the Earth was able to give us the resources and energy as per our exponential demands, we could fulfill any **Concept** and so were justified in feeling that anything is possible. We could cut as many forests as we wished, get as much metal to make as many tractors and draw as much oil to run them to get unlimited food from the Earth. We could get ourselves cars, planes, satellites, rockets – no limits to our imagination, concepts, dreams and desires. Yes, **Reality** was able to fulfill the requirement of the **Money Curve**.

Importantly, like the Runner, the Earth's body was able to deliver, so there appeared to be no damaging effects on the body of the Earth yet. These were **Paradise Times** and the sky was the limit. No wonder we felt we were destined to reach there.

38

PHASE 2 – Eco Collapse (Body Collapse)

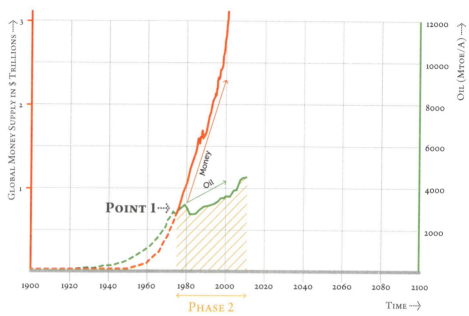

Starting **Phase 2** (early '70s) the 2 curves of **Concept** and **Reality** started moving apart. Money, by exponential definition wants to go steeply up, but Oil and all Natural resources follow the bell curve of the Earth which starts slowing down.

We now were in the same situation as the Runner whose body was not able to keep up with the exponential expectations of his coach. And just as his body started breaking down, so did the organic fabric of our Earth's body.

That was the **Beginning of the ECO-COLLAPSE**.

This breakdown was manifested in the first signs of species becoming extinct, forests disappearing, fisheries declining, rivers drying, aquifers depleting, etc.

Yet, intoxicated with our flurry of material success, we raced to a yet unknown point of departure at the top of the curve. We intensified our assault on the body of the Earth to feed the ever hungry and steeply rising Money Curve.

Phase 2
Body Collapse

So we cut half the world's forests...

strip-mined the earth...

blocked the earths arteries with 48,000 large dams...

diverted a quarter of the fresh water supplies for industries...

deprived other species of their rightful place in the web of life...

pushed them to extinction...

polluted our soil...

fabricated complex and unsustainable habitats like mega cities...

forged them to become financial centers of symbolic wealth...

and coerced everything that looked like a likely resource to come up with an edifice that we proudly called.......

Phase 2
Body Collapse

41

But how much of this can happen before the fabric of life starts unravelling visibly?

In Earth terms, this is called "exceeding the 'carrying capacity' of the Earth's ecosystems". Another way of saying we have crossed the limit beyond which the body of the Earth cannot repair itself and starts showing signs of stress and breakdown.

But we did not seem to care and we continued with our economic plans, thinking that their success was unconnected to the Earth's body matters.

Moreover, because in this phase the **Concept Curve** and **Reality Curve** drift apart, there is an unseen differential between projected gains and actual ones. So, invisible to all, the hollowness of growth was building up under the surface of financial systems (see diagram above).

Actually there were signs, fine cracks of failure, that showed up several times in this phase. Events that the world labelled as "bubbles" and were pretty much forgotten: the 1980 Japan asset price bubble, the 1997 Asian Crisis, the 2000 dot-com bubble… Despite these warnings we were not willing to see the emerging failure of the growth concept.

Every effort was made to deny reality and to perpetuate growth. This naturally made more demands on the body of the Earth and steadily

Phase 2
Body Collapse

43

accentuated the eco-collapse. But ironically, the more you damaged the body of the Earth, the more difficult it became to live up to the Money Curve and to the first principle of economics: the Time-Value of Money.

In 1981, E. F. Schumacher stated in his seminal book, *Small is Beautiful*:

> *"Modern man does not experience himself as a part of nature but as an outside force destined to dominate and conquer it. He even talks of a battle with nature, forgetting that, if he won the battle, he would find himself on the losing side".*

And that was exactly what we were to discover at the end of this phase.

Because, as time passed, and the two curves drifted exponentially apart, we found that besides certain life-systems fraying, so was our economic fabric weakening. We were finding it harder to match the Money Curve with real growth and, to match the deficit, the financial world had to float newer **Concepts** which would make the **Money Curve** appear true.

Remember that we had already defined money as a layer of **Concepts** with the intention of making it grow exponentially forever.

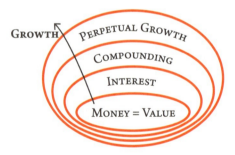

The prime mode of money growth is, therefore, through the mode of lending and charging a compounding interest. This is however restricted by how much money you can borrow. It is called **Liquidity**.

So instead of being limited to borrowing from individual people, we floated a new concept that would make it easy for us to borrow from thousands or even lakhs of investors to increase our Liquidity. This was done by selling shares in the enterprise that could be traded through an institutionalized system called the Stock Market. This marked the grand new entry of **Concept 5** in our layers of Money Concepts.

Concept 5: Stock Market

> **Reason:** It makes it easier to collect much larger capital from many more investors and therefore facilitates money growth even more.

But shares have 2 components – The **Dividend**, which is a real measure of productivity, and the **Share Price**, which is a perceived value. So that was the trick. With the deficit building up between the 2 curves, we needed to move onto perceived value because real growth was not keeping pace with the formula of exponential growth that we had imposed on our money system. In other words, we had become desperate enough to sanctify and institutionalise gambling.

Shares and Stock Markets of course existed before we reached phase 2 of the Money Curve, but the difference was that now they were being more broadly institutionalised as a mode of money growth.

However as time passed and the demands of the Money Curve rose ever steeper we needed to get more money into the system to keep it growing.

So we introduced **Concept 6** to increase Liquidity.

Concept 6: Fractional Reserve Banking: Allow the banks to lend a greater ratio of the capital they hold.

> **Reason:** It increased the amount of money that can be made available for loans which demand interest, of course. And interest is the prime mode of money expansion.

But this too reached a limit as eventually money was pegged to physical gold. So it was time for another Concept that would allow money to grow.

Concept 7: Remove the Gold Standard

> **Reason:** There is only so much gold. Therefore, if we only print money based on gold, we cannot increase the money base. This again hinders liquidity and therefore growth of money. Get rid of it for progress and development.

So the limiting ceiling to money, the Gold Standard, was unceremoniously removed in the U.S. by President Nixon in 1971. The dollar was reborn as a fiat currency that had no physical value to back it. More and more countries followed by adopting various diluted versions of the original full-reserve gold standard. The end of gold convertibility represented a

Phase 2
Body Collapse

fundamental change. From that point forward, the creation of U.S. dollars and, by extension, all of the world's currencies, was restrained by nothing more than political choice.

THE MONEY ONION

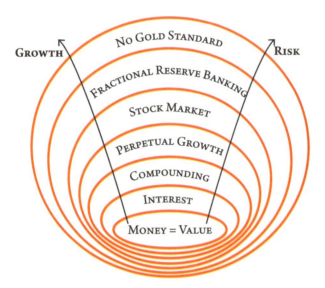

In short, we were shaping what I call the **Money Onion**. It consists of layers and layers of **Concepts** that can be extended outward at will by delving deeper into the mind and conjuring any number of symbolic ideas to add to the rules of money growth. Any real limits proving to be a hindrance to the exponential growth of money were being callously removed by the formulation of newer **Concepts**.

Yet there is a shadow side of the universe that counterbalances growth and profits – and that is **Risk**! With each added **Concept**, we were inadvertently underwriting a new level of risk. We would have to deal with this later.

For now, let us say that just like the Coach who did not tell the truth to his sponsors about the deficit building up between the projected and the actual speed of his trainee, we were shaping a financial system that was being less true to reflect actual growth or productivity and was getting more and more unstable and risky.

With each **Concept** added to remove a new limit to money growth, a new disconnect was accomplished between real production and value. We were truly shaping a casino model propped more and more on the perception and greed of investors and their speculation rather than representing any real growth of value. Yet we perceived growth of the value of money in just about everything from shares to services.

But remember the Money Curve is an exponential – starts slow then rises ever faster. By late '90s, the hunger of the Money Curve had so exploded that Fractional Reserve Banking and removing the Gold Standard were not enough, as they only remove the money ceiling. We still had to show ways in which it was growing – real or not. This was getting increasingly difficult.

Once more, what was needed was a new **Concept** which this time would not just raise the ceiling but could also act as a capital and asset multiplier. This was the concept of **Leverage**.

In physics, a lever is a device that allows you to lift a heavier weight with a smaller weight.

In finance, this was to be achieved by defining new instruments of investment that magnified profits with lesser investments.

Imagine putting down only 10,000 dollars that give you a stake on a million dollars. What about putting 1 million and getting leverage to 100 million?

And so, the world was gifted this new Concept of Leverage that promised a lot for a little.

Concept 8: Leverage: allows schemes where an investor or institution can use much more than the capital he owns.

> **Reason:** Well, why restrict enterprise? Money had proved to be a facilitator of growth so far and therefore we must have as much of it as possible in the system. That is the true path to progress and development.

But the well-known aspect of financial leverage is that, while it magnifies returns, it can also magnify risks disproportionately. The financial world did not fret as it felt secure that it already had an antidote for risks in the form of another **Concept** called **Options Trading**.

Options trading was a very old practice in the history of trading, used to minimize risk. Basically, options mean that a trader, who certainly does not know the future, could place an option to buy a stock at a later date at a predetermined, flat, up-front sum called a premium. If the stock went up, he had the option to buy at the agreed price BUT if the price dropped he only suffered the loss of the premium.

And so **Concept 9** of Options was added as a new layer to the Money Onion.

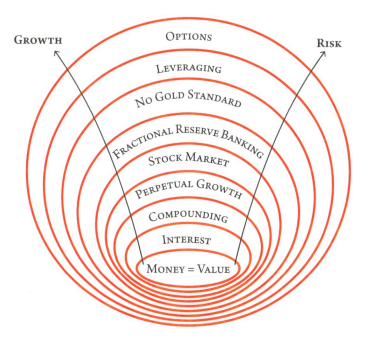

Concept 9: Options: provide an opportunity to leverage your capital for a bigger bet in the future against a minimal upfront commitment, called a premium.

Reason: Who wants risk? So if there is some way to minimize risk then this rule must be allowed.

This appeared to be a magic way to tame risk. The problem was no one knew how to price options – namely to set a fair premium amount to buy the option at.

This is where the math wizards came in. Fischer Black and Myron Scholes at MIT, Boston came up with a formula in 1973 that was to be known as the **Black-Scholes Options Pricing Formula** for minimizing risks in options.

$$C(S,t) = N(d_1)S - N(d_2)Ke^{-r(T-t)}$$

$$d_1 = \frac{1}{\sigma\sqrt{T-t}}\left[\ln\left(\frac{S}{K}\right) + \left(r + \frac{\sigma^2}{2}\right)(T-t)\right]$$

$$d_2 = \frac{1}{\sigma\sqrt{T-t}}\left[\ln\left(\frac{S}{K}\right) + \left(r - \frac{\sigma^2}{2}\right)(T-t)\right]$$

$$= d_1 - \sigma\sqrt{T-t}$$

$$P(S,t) = Ke^{-r(T-t)} - S + C(S,t)$$

$$= N(-d_2)Ke^{-r(T-t)} - N(-d_1)S$$

Source: Wikipedia

Above are a sample of the mind-numbing, complex equations, in terms of the Black-Scholes Options Pricing Formula that are used in financial models for an instrument called **Derivatives**.

Balancing the double-edge of Growth vs. Risk was getting treacherous. And yet, Derivatives, though immensely risky, were an insanely powerful multiplier of money. Only they could cope with this super steep part of the Money Curve. So again, helplessly, Derivatives joined the ranks of concepts in the Money Onion.

Concept 10: Derivatives: use all kinds of complex mathematical models to outwit reality.

> **Reason:** Well what is wrong with using mathematics to get an upper hand on reality? Only complex math promises to reduce risk. And the stakes are getting frighteningly high.

The very architects of derivatives were to discover what can go wrong with derivatives. Robert C. Merton and Myron Scholes won the 1997 Nobel prize for economics. They tested their model, by applying the Black-Scholes formula, in a financial investment firm called Long-Term Capital Management L. P. (LTCM) and raked billions. And then lost billions. Conveniently, the financial world forgave them their error. No one questioned the falseness of their mathematical model of perpetuating growth. It was put down to simply using their own formulae unwisely. The world concluded that since derivatives had worked like magic for a while, they could be made to do so again – as long as certain precautions were taken to deal with risk.

The truth was that Wall Street simply needed derivatives to keep the game of Growth going despite being well aware of the bloating Risk Factor. But their choice was to outwit it. They turned increasingly to MBAs, mathematicians and financial wizards from elite business schools to further use the power of mathematics to conquer risk.

But before **Concept 10** of derivatives could be applied on a grand scale, there was another road-block for banks. This was the Glass-Steagall Act of 1933 instilled by the U.S. Government which came into existence because of the risky practices of banks before the financial crash of 1929.

The crash was considered to be largely due to overzealous commercial bank involvement in stock market investment, which took on too much risk with depositors' money. In order to control this, the Glass-Steagall Act was setup as a regulatory firewall between commercial and investment bank activities. Banks were given a year to decide whether they would specialize in commercial or in investment banking. There was constant opposition to this act at all levels of the banking and financial community and some sections of the U.S. government. Yet, the Act remained firmly in place till 1995 for financial security reasons.

But nothing could hold back the demands of the Money Curve. Eventually, the Glass-Steagall Act was repealed in 1995. It was argued that it was seriously inhibiting growth. The repeal opened all stops and allowed big financial institutions to gamble with bank deposits and insurance funds at a colossal, institutionalized scale. Growth sky-rocketed but so did the Risk. This repeal was to be later acknowledged as the single largest factor in the 2008 financial crash.

Concept 11: **Repeal the Glass-Steagall Act**, and thereby remove control measures on banks.

> **Reason:** Allowing speculative instruments of investment with depositor funds was supposed to help banks generate unimaginable profits and therefore maintain exponential growth.

The combination of **Concept 10** (Derivatives) and **Concept 11** (Repealing the Glass Steagal Act) allowed the rampant creation of a plethora of **Concepts**. These were Hedge Funds, Credit Default Swaps, Collateralized Debt Obligation (CDO), Slice and Dice Mortgage, Structured Investment Vehicle (SIV) and many more **Concepts** collectively called **Complex Financial Instruments**. And layers and layers were added to the Money Onion.

Phase 2
Body Collapse

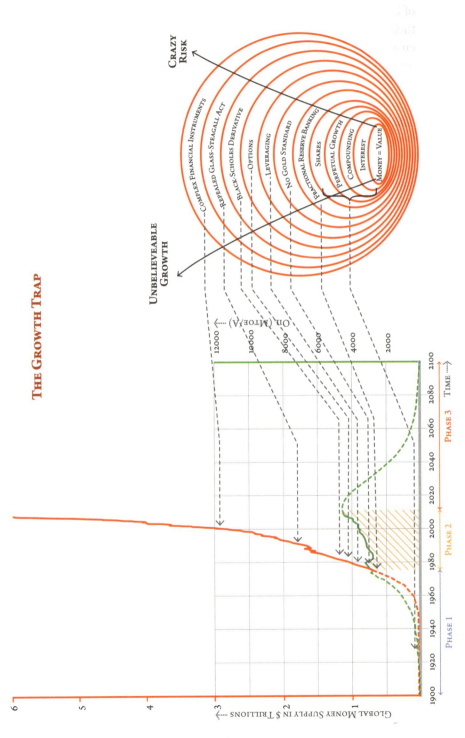

The Growth Trap

52

Concept 12: **Complex Financial Instruments** use derivatives to define risky paper financial instruments in such a manner that loans, mortgages and other financial transactions can be re-packaged and certified AAA, by colluding rating agencies and therefore can be sold as super-safe investments promising huge growth returns.

Reason: Well, let me think… I can't really think why we should have allowed such a blatant fraud. But then again, it was like injecting steroids into the growth machine. And, besides, it also gave homes to the uncredit-worthy all over the U.S. and investment options for the rest of the world, did it not? For a while at least.

Yes, these Complex Financial Instruments were behind the largest bubble in the history of the U.S. housing mortgages. And we all now know what happened to that in the year 2008. But while it worked it was a runaway success. All mortgaged houses were ATMs and any jobless citizen was a multiple house owner.

The Money Onion was flourishing. The diagram on the left, which I call **The Growth Trap**, shows the connection between the layers of the Money Onion and roughly the point in time on the **Concept/Money Curve** when we needed to institutionalize various concepts to sustain exponential growth of money.

Each layer added was stretching the **Concept** further into the mathematical realm of growth and each layer was adding another degree of risk from the unknown and the untested.

The profits were soaring, floating high above the **Reality Curve.** But the world was sweetly unaware of the dark forms that were morphing beneath these apparent gains.

Ironic that nobody questioned that derivatives are financial instruments that have no intrinsic value but "**derive**" their value from something else. Maybe it required a child to remind us that basically they are just bets. The funny thing about these bets is that you can bet both ways. You could bet that the price of something will go up and then (hedge your bet) by placing a side bet that it may go down. That is how "Hedge funds" hedge bets in the derivatives market. Even more, you can bet on just about anything from the price of commodities to currency values. And above all, there are no limits on the number of bets you can place.

Phase 2
Body Collapse

Now that is serious dabbling with real value. According to an article by Ellen Brown (*Global Research*, September 18, 2008):

> "'The point everyone misses,' *wrote economist Robert Chapman a decade ago, 'is that buying derivatives is not investing. It is gambling, insurance and high stakes bookmaking. Derivatives create nothing.' They not only create nothing, but they serve to enrich non-producers at the expense of the people who do create real goods and services.*"

This glaring discrepancy was amply illustrated in an article by Ian Stewart (Guardian News and Media Ltd. 2012):

> *"Black-Scholes underpinned massive economic growth. By 2007, the international financial system was trading derivatives valued at one quadrillion dollars per year. This is 10 times the total worth, adjusted for inflation, of all products made by the world's manufacturing industries over the last century".*

These mind boggling volumes of derivatives need to be put in perspective. Examine the bar graphs for some other well-known quantities in the year 2007:

- US Annual GDP is $14 trillion

- World GDP of all nations is $50 trillion

- Gross Global Industrial Production over the last 100 years is $100 trillion.

And Finally

- 2007 valuation of world derivatives was **$ 1000 trillion**

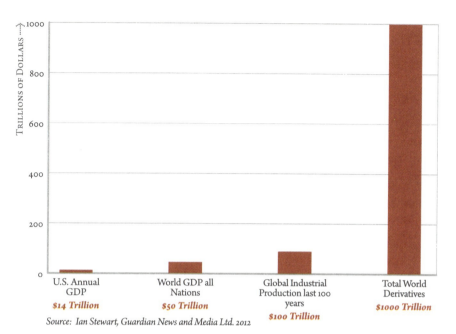

Source: Ian Stewart, Guardian News and Media Ltd. 2012

There you have it! The derivatives were supposed to be worth 10 times the total value of the world's industrial production over that last century! And nothing real to match that had been produced by what the derivatives represented. The gains were largely imaginary! The Money Onion was getting too large and hot to handle.

But right now, from the point of view of this book, I am not concerned with the ethics of the matter. My prime objective is to point out that this madness and illusive strategy was inevitable. This is an old pattern. We have done it at all previous stages of monetary growth – from the **Concept** of interest, to the compounding of interest, to shares, to mortgages, to options, to derivatives, to hedging, to complex financial instruments. Each new **Concept** adds another level of intensity to money growth. And an accompanying undertow of risk.

Therefore, in this case too, the creators of these crazy formulae and instruments were simply trying their best to live up to the exponential expectation of the **Money Curve**. That, after all, is the Holy Grail of our Modern Economic paradigm.

The only difference was that they were trying to achieve it by increasingly symbolic and dangerous means. In a sense, there was no way out for them but to perpetuate growth falsely, given that real production of real goods requires real resources and real energy from the body of the Earth. And we had long gone past that point.

Phase 2
Body Collapse

U.S. Treasury Secretary at the time, Henry Paulson, spoke about liquidity issues at Bear Stearns on television, saying *"the binding threads that run throughout these vast financial galaxies are derivatives, and the brightest minds on Wall Street worry about how they work – especially as stock markets around the world become more unpredictable and complex"*.

Warren Buffett, one of the world's richest business magnates, later called these risky, mathematical devices *"financial weapons of mass destruction"*.

Yes, these financial instruments were so complex that the very creators would later be unable to unravel them to figure out who was holding the can after the whole crazy scheme collapsed.

And collapse it certainly did!

In 2005, we reached **POINT 2:** the top of the **Reality Curve** (see diagram on opposite page).

This is the maximum amount of Oil that we can extract from the Earth. This point is called **Peak Oil.**

Oil is the ultimate key driver of industrial growth and reaching the Peak of Oil production was proving to be a death knell to the religion of **Perpetual Exponential Quantitative Growth** (**PEQG**).

The Peak of the Resource Curve marks the end of **Phase 2** which I have called **Body Collapse**. But as you can see, so far no one was seriously concerned about what was happening to the body of the Earth as long as our concept worked. But now the very **Concept** was in danger.

Because from **Point 2** onwards, the **Concept Curve** and the **Reality Curve** start moving in opposite directions. One wants to go up but the other simply goes down. The very concept of growth fails. This ensures the beginning of **Financial Collapse**, as a huge false value in the economy is waiting to be corrected permanently.

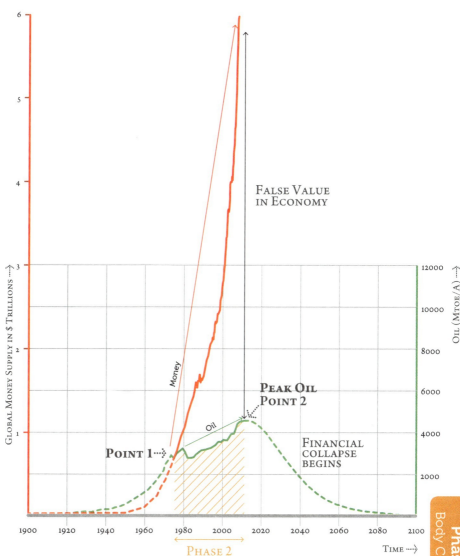

Civilization at large, and the financial pundits in particular, had made two fundamental but impossible assumptions:

- That the **Concept** was true: That growth was a God-given right and could be perpetuated with mere mental, financial and mathematical ingenuity.

- That **Reality** would support it: That energy and resources could be obtained at ever increasing speeds to maintain this growth.

The scary truth remained that their model was like a ball of wool with one loose end tucked inside. No matter how deep inside the loose end is hidden, it will unravel one day.

And that loose end started unravelling unnoticed around 2005, when the world reached the Peak of Oil production.

From 2005 onwards, with each passing moment, the lie between **Concept** and **Reality** became harder to contain. Oil prices shot to $146 per barrel and the Financial System, predicated on cheap energy, collapsed in 2008. In a short period of a few months, **50 trillion** dollars of perceived money got wiped off the world balance sheets.

This was **Reality** correcting the record.

We had reached the end of Phase 2, which marks the Beginning of FINANCIAL COLLAPSE.

This is the iron-clad proof of Peak Oil and just a preview of what is to follow. A lot more imaginary money is lurking in pseudo assets below the surface waiting to get corrected in Phase 3 on the downside of the **Reality Curve** of Energy Descent!

"Anyone who believes that exponential growth can go on forever in a finite world is either a madman or an economist".

Kenneth Ewart Boulding - economist, educator, and interdisciplinary philosopher

PHASE 3 – Financial Collapse (Concept Collapse)

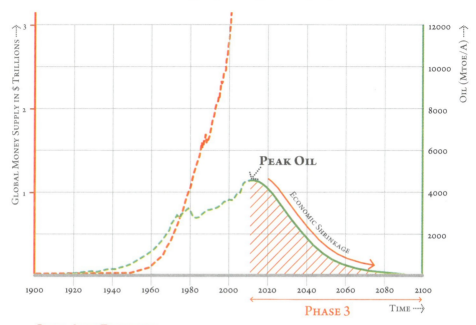

STOP AND REFLECT:

We are today perched at the top of the **Reality Curve** – the Peak of Oil production that drives our concept of financial growth. Modern Industrial Civilization has therefore reached the limits of its **Concept**.

The future path in **Phase 3** seems steeply downhill with our current economic paradigm.

This is a good time to reflect.

Remember that we were in a similar situation with the Super Coach and the Runner. A crazy concept of the Super Coach to ever exponentially increase the speed of the Runner leads to the burning of all aspects of his health capital: body fitness, mental stability, social relationships and spiritual integrity. The cumulative effect is the collapse of his Body followed by the collapse of the Coach's **Concept**.

Similarly, a crazy and unreal concept of Perpetual Exponential Quantitative Growth of money leads to chasing and looting half the planet's energy and resources, disrupting ecosystems, fraying social structures and corrupting moral integrity. The sum crisis is double edged again – deterioration of **Health** and finally **Wealth**.

Inspired by Charles Eisenstein's book *The Ascent of Humanity* I have re-categorised the **Health Capital** of the Earth as a living organism. I divide them as follows:

- **Natural Capital** - inanimate items useful to man – fuels such as coal, oil and natural gas, and materials such as timber, metal ores, limestone, salt, slate, clay, chalk, gypsum, silica, arable land etc.

- **Ecological Capital** - the living fabric of the planet – forests, rivers, plant kingdom, animal kingdom, microbes etc.

- **Social Capital** - the bonds in family, community and society between people: love, respect, mutual caring, peace and harmony.

- **Cultural Capital** - folklore, dance forms, music, songs, arts and ideas that form a community knowledge base.

- **Spiritual Capital** - the beliefs, morals, ethics and values of a society such as honesty, faith and trust.

We see **Health** (all kinds of Body capital) and **Wealth** (Financial Capital) as two separate entities but they are related in an ironic fashion. Over the span of the Modern Industrial Age, our economic paradigm of perpetual growth has effectively burnt most of this cumulative **Health Capital** with the sole objective of converting it to **Financial Capital**.

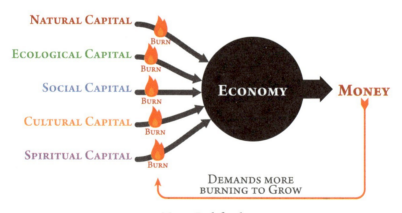

Money Redefined

Natural Capital, like fossil fuels, was extracted to be used to build and run machines that would destroy **Ecological Capital** such as forests, rivers and eco systems to shape the modern industrial world where the **Social Capital** of peoples health, peace and habits were changed, from family and community pursuits, to mere round-the-clock production staking claim to common **Cultural Capital**, all with the intention of converting to a single symbolic form of capital called Money. This constant chasing of money and profits against impossible growth targets in the face of depleting resources built up pressures to burn the **Spiritual Capital** of honesty, integrity, and loyalty of people.

And the only thing that burning creates is a symbolic token called Money that is nothing but a lubricant and facilitator to perpetuate the creation of more tokens in a system that we call Modern Economics. Money is not value but a catalyst that makes the scheme of perpetual growth possible. And is it really proving useful?

Look at the state of the world around and you get the answer.

But like I said at the beginning of this book, I am not directly addressing morality but "possibility". Of course it is a bad idea to burn all kinds of capital that is irreplaceable and vital to life to create a worthless token that demands more of the same. Yet in this book, I focus on the fact that much as we may want and decide to run the current economic paradigm, we will simply NOT be able to so. Because the key resource that permitted us to do this happens to be oil. And Peak Oil spells an end to these plans.

The world of Business and Finance particularly needs to be aware of Peak Oil, because the 2008 collapse of the global financial system was the direct consequence of ignoring the peaking of Earth's key and most precious resource: Oil.

This is the highest point in the **Reality Curve**. The maximum amount of oil the Earth will give us at a point in time. This is a geological limit and nothing or no one can change it. This is the turning point. From here we start an inverted journey back to Earth because all capital from the Earth is eventually governed by rules of the **Reality Curve**, which is a Bell Curve. And ironically, even oil, our key industrial resource, religiously follows this curve.

And so no matter how hard we try to feed the Money Curve, the Earth will follow the Bell Curve and cannot be made to fulfill the exponential curve of economic expectation. These are early rumblings of Peak Oil – a phenomenon the world will humbly have to understand and accept.

Economics should therefore be a holistic and sensitive science to manage all the **Natural**, **Ecological**, **Social**, **Cultural** and **Spiritual** capital

Phase 3
Concept Collapse

we have inherited. Instead we have morphed the Laws of Economics to transcend and override all these.

To verify what I am saying, please follow any article in the newspapers, or debate on television, on the 2008 financial collapse and the subsequent recession. You will only find complex and erudite arguments, by deluded economic experts, all trying to wrestle with the crisis using a plethora of financial terms: capital, debt, equity, loan, subsidy and so on. All symbolic representations of value but not value in themselves. These are followed by phrases like "slowing growth", "spiralling inflation", "a collapsing currency", "a burgeoning fiscal deficit", "structural liquidity shortage" and "a hostile external economic environment".

There is no mention of any real value on which money is based. No mention of the principles of energy or depletion of resources or Peak Oil. They are ever wishing the infinite and denying the finite. That is how deluded we in general, and the financial world in particular, have become.

Much like the Super Coach, our economists arrogantly believe that it is all about their Super Concept of money and growth that runs the world. They both believe that only the rigors of their method will make the Runner/Economy achieve their conceptual but impossible goal of eternal quantitative growth.

While the Super Coach was hell bent on killing his Runner for his concept, we are committed to doing the same to Mother Earth with our concept of Perpetual Exponential Quantitative Growth (PEQG).

Once more we are at the same crossroads. We are at the peak of performance and peak of resource consumption. Yet speed and size is no indicator of the stability and security of the future. Much as how an object dropped from a height is fastest just before it hits the ground!

How the future of **Money** (Concept, Mind) and **Earth** (Reality, Body) pans out in **Phase 3**, which is starting now, depends on the changes we make to our paradigm and what choices we make. But if you were to ask me, then this is what I would say once again.

We must do two things, very similar to the Super Coach and the Runner, at this point of time.

1. Kill the Concept
Namely abandon the crazy Concept of Perpetual Exponential Financial Growth. It was impossible anyway and even more hazardous in the light of Peak Oil.

2. Save the Body
Stop pumping the Earth's body with aggressively desperate measures of Modern Industrial Development that burn all forms of Capital to perpetuate the impossible expectation of Perpetual Money Growth. Or else, we and the living fabric of the Earth will die prematurely and painfully.

Or would you rather have it the other way – Save the Concept of Perpetual Exponential Quantitative Growth and Kill the Earth's Body?

I know what I would opt for, but this time it is not an individual choice. The choice has to be unanimously ours. It is our collective Body. The Earth is an extension of all our bodies.

Or wait a minute!

Maybe ironically this time the choice is NOT left to us.

The Earth will decide how much growth is possible.

With the Peaking of Oil production we have also reached the Peak of Growth.

To understand Peak Oil and its nonnegotiable implications on the Financial and Modern Industrial World we will move to PART II of this book.

"Until you change the way money works, you change nothing".

M. King Hubbert, Ph.D. - Geologist who accurately predicted U.S. and Global Peak Oil

Phase 3
Concept Collapse

The Disease & the Trigger

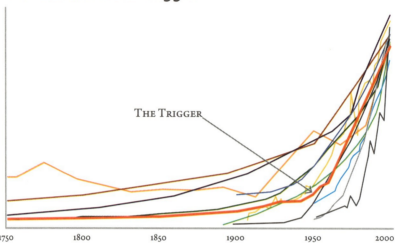

THE TRIGGER

| 1750 | 1800 | 1850 | 1900 | 1950 | 2000 |

One last thing before we end this section and go to Part II of this book.

Imagine that the collection of graphs shown above are of the vital signs of the health of a patient who is in an Intensive Care Unit.

The graphs show his heart rate, blood pressure, body temperature, blood sugar level, cholesterol level and other vital signs of health. There is an optimum level or a narrow band within which each of these vital signs should be if the patient is to be deemed healthy.

The one thing you notice is that all the vital signs are shooting up exponentially. The patient's blood pressure is shooting off the chart in an exponential fashion. And so are his heart rate and body temperature and blood sugar level and cholesterol level. All the vital signs are haywire and increasing exponentially. What would you say is happening to the patient?

Well, I don't need to be an M.D. to tell you that the poor patient is pretty close to dying.

But what if I told you this patient in ICU is actually our planet, Mother Earth?

Yes, and these graphs are from ACTUAL figures that represent the vital signs of the Earth's health.

• *Loss of tropical rain forests and woodland* - going up exponentially.

• *Species extinction* - going up exponentially.

64

- *Fisheries exploited* - going up exponentially.

- *Water usage* - going up exponentially.

- *Number of motor cars* - going up exponentially.

- *CO2 concentration* - going up exponentially.

- *Northern Hemisphere average temperatures* - going up exponentially.

- *Ozone depletion* - going up exponentially.

- *Paper consumption* - going up exponentially.

- *Population* - going up exponentially.

There are many more such vital signs that are going up exponentially but we cannot mention them all here. What is more important is indeed that they are all going up in an exponential manner.

Hidden amongst all these graphs is one very important graph marked by the arrow '**The Trigger**'.

This graph is the *GDP of The World (RED)*. And that too is going up exponentially.

But that is what we wanted, did we not, when we made the rules of Money?

Remember we said "Money has Time-Value".

Money must Grow.

This growth must compound.

Year after year. Decade after decade. Century after century. Ad infinitum!!!

That is what we call our economic goal, don't we?

That is what we call progress and development, don't we?

That is the yardstick against which we measure anything that is worth doing in life, is it not?

That then is Perpetual Exponential Quantitative Growth.

That is our Economic Law.

THEN that crazy law is in fact THE TRIGGER. That is what is causing all other health signs of our Mother Earth to go up exponentially.

So what would you say is happening to this patient?

The patient is dying for sure. THE EARTH IS DYING!!!!

The Diagnosis:

- OUR CRAZY CONCEPT OF EXPONENTIAL GROWTH OF MONEY HAS SUCCEEDED IN SHAPING OUR ECONOMIC GDP CURVE EXPONENTIALLY

- BUT HAS RESULTED IN DESTRUCTION OF HEALTH CAPITAL EXPONENTIALLY

- REFLECTED IN ALL EARTH'S LIFE SIGNS GOING UP EXPONENTIALLY

- BRINGING ALL OUR LIFE SYSTEMS UNDER SERIOUS THREAT!

And all because of our insistence on a false Economic Paradigm called GROWTH.

Perpetual Exponential Quantitative Growth to be exact.

The kind that reaches for the SKY at the cost of the EARTH!

But the Earth has an ace up her sleeve to correct our little delusion.

That ace, which is just about to trump our crazy economic dreams of perpetual growth, is called PEAK OIL.

The next chapter is all about this reality.

Welcome to Peak Oil.

"Growth for the sake of growth is the ideology of the cancer cell".

Edward Abbey - American writer noted for his advocacy of environmental issues and criticism of public land policies

Part II

Peak Oil
The Perpetual Growth Myth under Siege

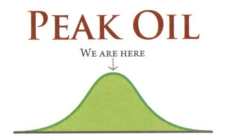

PEAK OIL
WE ARE HERE

To understand the true implications of Peak Oil, it is crucial that we identify the key aspects of our situation.

We are looking at:

The Future of a *Modern Industrial Society*

in the face of reaching *The Peak*

of a key *Finite Non-Renewable Energy Resource*

in the context of

Perpetual Exponential Quantitative Growth.

Peak Means Half Gone

Yes, that is the most amazing thing about Peak Oil. We have to worry about oil when it is only half gone. Yes, there is still half the oil left but everything changes at the halfway point. Especially for economics.

To wake up to the true implications of Peak Oil, it is critical that we focus on each line of the definition (on the opposite page) individually.

- The key is that the peak is dangerous to our Modern Industrial Society and not to an agrarian society which, in any case, was not heavily dependent on oil.

- The truth is that reaching the half-way point is itself vital because beyond that point, the resource only declines.

- The fact is that Oil is a "key finite non-renewable energy resource" and NOTHING can replace it.

- And finally, no other resource or combination of resources can keep up with this expectation of Perpetual Exponential Quantitative Growth (PEQG).

Only when we understand these points, individually and cumulatively, will we understand Peak Oil and the crunch that we are in.

150 MILLION YEARS OF THE SUN'S ENERGY....

CRUDE OIL

.... HALF GONE IN 150 YEARS.

Modern Industrial World

Let us start with the Modern Industrial World. What is it actually?

To most, the Modern Industrial World is the epitome of man's ingenuity: a glorious manifestation of human intelligence and enterprise.

In my opinion, this is completely untrue.

The fact is that all the seemingly fabulous constructs and conveniences of the Modern Industrial World were only possible because of abundant and cheap fossil fuels. Human ingenuity was a co-factor and not the prime reason for it. As simple as that!

With a wild Concept like "Time-Value of Money" floating on the edge of our consciousness, we were simply looking for the perfect ally from Reality to make Exponential Growth possible.

And we found that ally.

It was Oil – nothing but over 150 million years of ancient sunlight trapped in the bosom of the Earth.

A once-in-an-eternity bounty. Plentiful, cheap, energy-dense, portable, easily convertible to heat, motion, and electricity… A primeval elixir so varied in possibilities, having the unique innate ability to morph into a dazzling array of useful materials that it, but naturally, shaped the most powerful culture ever to dominate this Earth: modern industrial civilization.

No wonder oil has been referred to as the "blood of the devil", a double-edged warning.

With the discovery of oil, the Concept and the Reality fused effortlessly and we took the easiest path. Whatever oil offered us, we seized: cars, air-planes, plastics, lubricants, complex electronics, computers, space travel, internet, gigabyte memory chips, mobile networks, artificial limbs, mega cities, automated garbage collection, robot-controlled assembly lines, global food networks, moving mountains or damming rivers, clearing forests or strip mining!

Anything seemed possible! Nothing else could have achieved it on this scale of size, speed and complexity. Yes, oil allowed us to nurture the most audacious, wasteful, self-indulgent and even self-destructive ideas we could dream about, and turn them into reality.

This led the civilized world to believe that we did all this because of our superior intelligence as a species and as a culture. We patted ourselves on the back by terming it innate "human ingenuity". We felt that, even if oil was removed or reduced, we could simply replace it with some other form of energy and continue on the same trajectory. This we also deemed to be our entitlement and inevitable destiny.

Shoot the messenger but the message remains. This is a pipe-dream.

Few ponder on why this is so.

It is because oil was not only an unbelievably cheap, plentiful, dense and portable source of energy to RUN our world, but also a divinely unique source of mind-boggling byproducts that BUILT our Modern Industrial World. Bitumen for our roads, plastics for everything, lubricants for all kinds of machinery, fertilizers and pesticides for our complex and vulnerable modern food production, chemical reagents for pharmaceuticals and endlessly more.

All these and more are intertwined in a complex web of interdependencies that are hard to unravel, let alone replace, to make the Modern Industrial World possible.

And reaching the peak of oil production means only an imminent decline of what is possible.

The world will not disappear because of Peak Oil but we will find ourselves in a considerably different world with a new set of economic rules, in fact, an inversion of the rules of Economics: Shrinkage instead of Growth.

To appreciate fully what oil means, we first have to do a primer on energy.

Energy - The Universal Currency

The primary source of energy that is vital to us is the sun.

Through a miraculous process called photosynthesis, the sun's energy is captured as carbohydrates by plants. And over millennia it has shaped the stunning beauty and complexity of life manifested in our ecosystems.

The accumulation and compression of these layers of life over eons have resulted in all the combustible fossil fuels that we take so much for granted. By fossil fuels we mean oil, coal and natural gas which form 87% of our total energy consumption.

We must remind ourselves that these fossil fuels are nothing but a humongous savings account of ancient sunlight that we are tapping into at a maddening pace – millions of times faster than it can be generated.

In short, we have taken 150 million years of sunlight and burnt half of it in just 150 years.

This is equivalent to spending 500,000 times your salary every month!

Hardly the kind of wisdom any course on economics would advocate. But then Economics was only considered with accounting for money. What we now have to learn is the deeper and more crucial kind of accounting called **Energy Accounting**. This is because energy is the true currency of the universe and not money.

In this scale of energy needed, there is really no other source of energy worth mentioning that can match or fulfil the demands of our Modern Industrial World.

In Chapter 3, we explore principles for energy accounting that are vital for us to honestly evaluate where we stand.

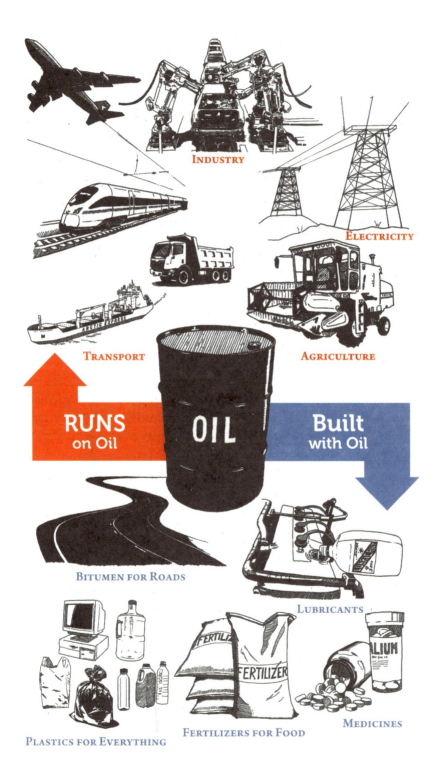

INDUSTRY

ELECTRICITY

TRANSPORT

AGRICULTURE

RUNS on Oil

OIL

Built with Oil

BITUMEN FOR ROADS

LUBRICANTS

PLASTICS FOR EVERYTHING

FERTILIZERS FOR FOOD

MEDICINES

Uniqueness of Oil
Running vs. Building

What part of our oil is running the world and what part is building it?

Energy Component: RUNNING

From 1 barrel of oil of 42 gallons, only 32 gallons of gasoline, diesel and jet fuel for transportation, etc. goes towards running our Modern Industrial World by moving our cars, trucks, trains, planes, machines etc.

Byproduct Component: BUILDING

The remaining 10 gallons per barrel are used to make products such as plastics, lubricants, bitumen, fertilizers, etc. that are crucial to building the fabric of the Modern Industrial World.

Please dwell a bit on the information above. The core point is easily missed when we think that oil is mainly a form of energy that moves things around or RUNS the world. Because in fact, about a third of each barrel of oil actually goes to BUILD and MAINTAIN the very fabric of our industrial world.

Yes, 33% of the barrel of oil goes into making unique oil-based products like bitumen, plastics, fertilizers, lubricants, pharmaceuticals, etc. that we cannot get from any other source of energy. Not solar, not windmills, not nuclear, nor anything else. In fact, all so-called alternative energy options are themselves built using oil energy and byproducts.

Besides, what do solar, windmills, nuclear, fuel cells, etc. give you in the end? Only electricity!

None of them give you liquid fuels and the truth is that our world does not run on electricity but it runs on Liquid Fuels that come mainly from oil. We will elaborate on this later in Part III of this book on **Alternative Energies**.

The long and short of it is that the world RUNS on oil and the world is BUILT with oil. This cannot be said about any other source of energy. Oil is irreplaceable in the way we have built our Modern Industrial World.

The energy component of oil RUNS the manufacturing and transport of all kinds of goods, and helps to start and run businesses all around the globe. BUT it is bitumen, the byproduct component of oil, which is used to build the roads that all transportation networks need. No other source

75

of energy can give us these byproducts.

The energy component of oil generates electricity BUT the byproduct component of oil provides insulators, plastics, a heavier grade of oil for cooling transformers, etc. that have built the electrical infrastructure and large parts of the electronic industry. No other source of energy can give us these byproducts.

With the energy component of oil, we shaped systems to grow excess food of all kinds, needed or not. This we did through aggressive and wasteful agricultural practices that required increasing the amount of oil used to grow, irrigate, and harvest, with an increasing number of machines and industrial methods. We then processed this food with oil energy in thousands of ways, healthy or not, and then transported the processed foods to far-flung corners of the globe. BUT the byproduct component of oil provided the fertilizers that made this kind of energy-intensive agriculture possible. No other source can give us fertilizers as byproducts so cheap and plentiful.

What we proudly dubbed the "green revolution" was nothing but industrial, fossil-fueled agriculture using mono-cropping techniques. To maintain present levels of food production, oil is needed right from plowing to spraying fertilizers and pesticides to cropping to thrashing to cleaning to packing to storing to transporting to refrigeration... till it reaches your neighborhood supermarket. Remove oil from this network and the complete food system will collapse.

The food we get today is grown with oil used for fertilizers, herbicides, pesticides, irrigation and harvesting. This food is then transported over an average of 1200 miles.

In the United States, about ten calories of hydrocarbon energy are required to produce one calorie of food.

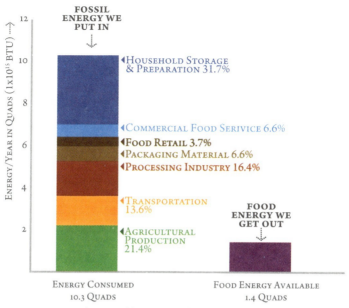

Source: *Center for Sustainable Systems Newsletter - US Food System Factsheets*

The diagram above shows a comparison of oil energy that we put into growing our food (left bar) and the much lower energy that the food actually gives us (right bar). The ratio of energy put in against what you get out is 10:1. So you are eating petroleum not sunshine. The more advanced a country is in modern agriculture, the higher the ratio of petroleum energy to sunshine in your food.

And finally the killer effect! Because fossil fuels made intensive agriculture possible, excess food translated into increased population in an exponential manner, doubling ever faster till it reached 7 billion. The one simple ecological fact that most people don't know is that it does not matter which species it is, the ecological rule is - more food means more population. And, at a core level, we humans also follow ecological rules, like all other living organisms.

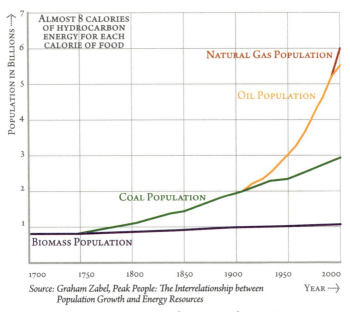

Source: Graham Zabel, Peak People: The Interrelationship between Population Growth and Energy Resources

If we were to only rely on bio-mass (blue graph), which is the sun's energy converted to plants, the world population would be around 800 million. But then we discovered coal (green graph), the first fossil fuel to kickstart fossil-fuel based, intensive agriculture and therefore exponential growth of population. Then oil (yellow graph) and then natural gas (red graph) took the population to over 7 billion in 2011. This is exponential growth of population following exponential growth of fossil fuel energy used in our modern agricultural system.

Apart from burning fossil fuel, the growth of modern agriculture has usurped 40% of the Earth's photosynthetic capacity by converting numerous natural ecosystems into farm land. This has seriously debilitated the ecological systems that are crucial for climate stability and has brought the heightened extinction of non-human species.

Several studies show that the U.S. is so dependent on fossil fuel for its agriculture, that it would be incapable of sustaining more than about two-thirds of its population today without fossil fuel. If we think about this at a global scale, only an estimated 2 billion people would be able to live in a world without fossil fuel.

Taking all of this into account, we see how a world based on oil-based agriculture that is facing Peak Oil would mean less food. And less food would bring a decrease in population.

A.A. Bartlett, Prof. Emeritus of Physics, Univ. of Colorado, Boulder has rightfully said:

"Modern agriculture is the use of land to convert petroleum into food".

Dependency on Oil's Byproducts

Check this list out. These are but a few of the 6000 items that are dependent on the byproducts of oil. *(Source: Ranken-energy.com)*

Ammonia, Anesthetics, Antihistamines, Artificial limbs, Artificial Turf, Antiseptics, Aspirin, Auto Parts, Awnings, Balloons, Ballpoint pens, Bandages, Beach Umbrellas, Boats, Cameras, Candles, Car Battery Cases, Carpets, Caulking, Combs, Cortisones, Cosmetics, Crayons, Credit Cards, Curtains, Deodorants, Detergents, Dice, Disposable Diapers, Dolls, Dyes, Eye Glasses, Electrical Wiring Insulation, Faucet Washers, Fishing Rods, Fishing Line, Fishing Lures, Food Preservatives, Food Packaging, Garden Hose, Glue, Hair Coloring, Hair Curlers, Hand Lotion, Hearing Aids, Heart Valves, Ink, Insect Repellent, Insecticides, Linoleum, Lipstick, Milk Jugs, Nail Polish, Oil Filters, Panty Hose, Perfume, Petroleum Jelly, Rubber Cement, Rubbing Alcohol, Shampoo, Shaving Cream, Shoes, Toothpaste, Trash Bags, Upholstery, Vitamin Capsules, Water Pipes, Yarn, Solvents, Diesel fuel, Motor Oil, Bearing Grease, Ink, Floor Wax, Football Cleats, Sweaters, Insecticides, Bicycle Tires, Sports Car Bodies, Dresses, Tires, Golf Bags, Cassettes, Dishwasher Parts, Tool Boxes, Shoe Polish, Motorcycle Helmet, Transparent Tape, CD Player, Faucet Washers, Clothesline, Basketballs, Soap, Purses, Dashboards, Footballs, Putty, Refrigerant, Percolators, Life Jackets, Linings, Skis, TV Cabinets, Shag Rugs, Electrician's Tape, Tool Racks, Epoxy, Paint, Mops, Slacks, Insect Repellent, Umbrellas, Fertilizers, Roofing, Toilet Seats, Denture Adhesive, Ice Cube Trays, Synthetic Rubber, Speakers, Plastic Wood, Electric Blankets, Glycerin, Tennis Rackets, Rubber, Cement, Fishing Boots, Nylon Rope, House Paint, Roller Skates, Surf Boards, Wheels, Rollers, Shower Curtains, Guitar Strings, Luggage, Safety Glasses, Antifreeze, Football Helmets, Clothes, Toothbrushes, Ice Chests, Combs, CDs & DVDs, Paint Brushes, Vaporizers, Sun Glasses, Tents, Heart Valves, Parachutes, Telephones, Enamel, Pillows, Dishes, Dentures, Model Cars, Folding Doors, Cold cream, Movie Film, Soft Contact Lenses, Drinking Cups, Fan Belts, Car Enamel, Refrigerators, Golf Balls, Petrol.

Complex Web of Oil Inter-Dependencies

Beyond the surface level of dependencies comes the more scary and dark reality of Inter-dependencies. How one product or facet of oil is connected to another and another and another in an ever-widening web of inter-dependencies. It opens a Pandora's box.

But just for discussion's sake, it could make a mind-boggling game.

So let us take a simple item like a ball point pen. How does oil feature in it? Well, for a start, all the plastic of the refill is a byproduct of oil. And then all the non-plastic components were extracted using oil based machinery, then transported using oil to factories that were built with oil. The ink is made using solvents, including toluene and propyl alcohol that are byproducts from coal and oil processing.

Now go to the next level. Where was the plastic refill made? In a factory, of course. And where were the machines in those factories made? In other factories. And each one has infrastructure and machines that were built using oil energy. The electricity for most of these places was generated by burning coal, which is again a fossil fuel, like oil.

And how do the people who run these factories come to work? In cars that run on oil. And how were those cars manufactured? In factories that run on oil of course. And what about the parts and machinery to make those factories? They came from other factories that are built with oil, of course.

And where do these people who work in these factories live? In houses that were built using...

Try playing this game seriously for as long as you can. You will realize that it is an ever-widening web of oil interdependencies so hard to unravel that you can forget about replacing oil with any alternative. The more complicated a gadget is, the more the industries and processes involved in fabricating it. Each industry and process is linked in complex ways to oil and its byproducts.

There is only one outcome if you do this honestly. You will realize why the Modern Industrial World is doomed at the slightest decline in oil production.

This is only a brief description of what it takes to maintain the Modern Industrial World. Every facet of it is an artifact of cheap and abundant petroleum energy and its byproducts. We are enmeshed in our dependency on oil and its byproducts to such a degree that it is frightening to even examine the subject in its totality.

The Peak – Hubbert's Curve

Now that you have realized how CRUCIAL oil is to the running and building of our Modern Industrial World, we may better examine in what pattern it depletes.

Oil Wells and the Bell Curve

How do oil wells behave? In other words, how fast or how much oil do they give us over time?

The most common and false perception is that an oil well is like a huge underground tank from which we can extract oil at will (limited only by the size of the pump and the capacity of that well of course). This has been proved to be untrue.

M. King Hubbert
1903 - 1989

Oil, being viscous, takes time to move through pores and crevices in the rock that contains it. Therefore, extracting and producing oil follows a distinct pattern.

The distinct and unchanging behavior of all oil wells was discovered by Marion King Hubbert, a geoscientist working at the Shell research lab in Houston, Texas, in the early 1950s.

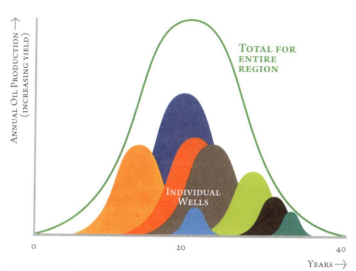

Hubbert predicted that the rate of oil production resembles a Bell Curve as shown here.

Whether it be a single well…
Or a given geographical area…
Or the planet as a whole.

No longer could we assume that we could just pump out oil at whatever rate we wished. The oil well would decide it for us.

And the output was in the shape of the bell curve which I introduced you to at the beginning as the **Reality Curve**.

The key points of oil production in a Bell Curve pattern are:

1. It does not matter how large the well is, it will always follow the shape of the **bell curve**.

2. The maximum rate of extraction of oil or **The Peak** happens at the **mid-way point**, when you have taken out ONLY half of the oil from that well. And from there it only goes down.

3. This is true for one well as much as for all the wells in production at a point of time.

Wow! Now this was an amazing game changer, both for the petroleum industry and for the industrial world at large. To start getting less and less oil starting at only the **HALF-WAY** point is a calamity. Especially because we believe in perpetual exponential growth, and that requires that we are able to draw more and more oil from the Earth at whatever speed we choose. This is impossible after the half-way point, as per Hubbert's discovery.

Based on his theory, he presented a paper at the 1956 meeting of the American Petroleum Institute in San Antonio, Texas, which predicted that the United States petroleum production would peak between the late 1960s and the early 1970s and then start a permanent decline. Meaning, the U.S. would thereafter produce less and less oil each year. And so growth of industry could only decline in the U.S. after that peak.

No wonder Hubbert met with such scathing criticism at first. He was mocked and ridiculed. To be proved right, Hubbert had a long and lonely wait from 1956 onwards.

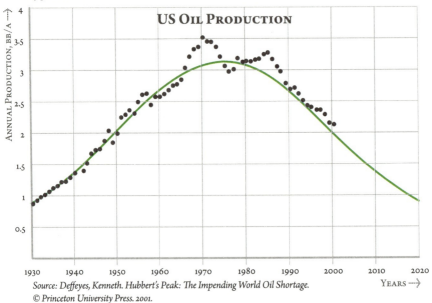

Source: Deffeyes, Kenneth. Hubbert's Peak: The Impending World Oil Shortage.
© Princeton University Press. 2001.

In 1971, U.S. oil production peaked as predicted by him as per the graph above.

Oil production peaked and began to decline regardless of surrealistic technological progress, extensive investment and U.S. tax policies that would hand over a trillion dollars to the American oil industry trying to keep it afloat.

This brought about a new era in U.S. history, where expanding its search for oil outside its borders became paramount in order to maintain the country's growth rate.

Hubbert became famous and celebrated.

Hubbert's Curve was no longer a theory. It was now a geological law!

How did Hubbert Predict U.S. Peak Oil?

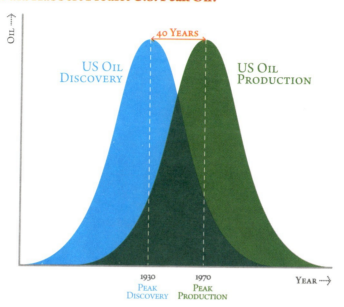

Hubbert was not a fortune teller. He was a scientist specializing in geology. He did a statistical analysis based on data regarding Discoveries vs. Production of Oil within the U.S.

From the data of oil wells within a region, he knew that the time between the discovery and production peaks would be approximately 40 years.

And so, when he expanded this to the whole of the U.S. and noticed that the total U.S. oil discoveries had peaked in 1930, he was able to extrapolate and predict that the peak of oil production for petroleum in the U.S. would be about 40 years into the future, which would be in 1970.

He however had to wait a while till 1956 to verify the actual facts before he made the announcement.

And indeed, U.S. oil production did peak around 1971.

World Peak Oil

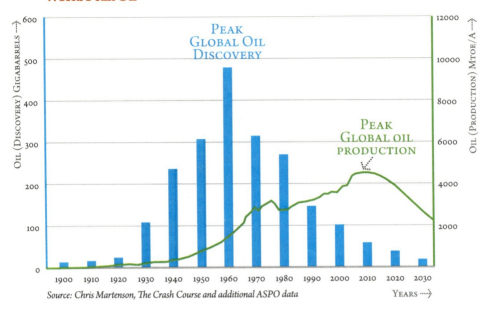

Source: Chris Martenson, The Crash Course and additional ASPO data

Similarly, to predict when the total world oil production would peak, Hubbert had to wait a bit longer. This is because he had to wait for the peak of global oil discoveries to occur.

And this happened in the 1960s. Based on that, in 1974 he projected that global oil production would peak 40 years later, between 1995 and 2000.

The peak, in fact, was delayed several years because of a political setback called the Arab Oil Embargo, when the oil producing countries of the Middle East withheld oil from the rest of the world for a couple of years. As a result, much less oil was consumed globally in the seventies. Nevertheless, world oil production did finally peak around 2005.

And ever since, we have been at the top of the curve at roughly 85 to 86 million barrels/day. This is the Global Peak of Oil production. No new areas are able to compensate the decreasing oil supply and there is unfortunately no escape from experiencing the impacts of Peak Oil.

It is also shaping up so far as a bell curve all the way from the beginning to the top. These are real annual figures of total world oil production plotted on a graph. The future shape is projected from past experiences, but the rate of decline obviously depends on our future consumption patterns.

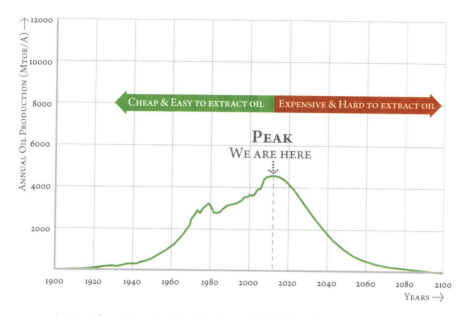

Let us take a closer look at the **Actual Global Oil Production** curve and see what it tells us.

This is the Actual Reality Curve. Note how it approximately looks similar to a bell curve.

This curve is making the GDP growth possible. We are at the top of the Oil Production curve at present and have been since 2005. The top in fact looks like a wavy, bumpy plateau. The vertical dotted line down the middle denotes our position in 2012: 84 to 86 Million Barrels per day.

This is the end of **Phase 2**, and can only mean the beginning of financial contraction. Pretty much what we are seeing unfolding all around the globe.

Good old supply and demand concepts of classical economics kicked in from 2005 when we hit the peak and oil started its steep increase in price. Despite oil reaching an all-time high of $146 per barrel in 2007, the world's oil producing countries and OPEC were unable to increase their outputs.

Despite the fact that countries depending on oil implored for more, oil producers failed to increase their oil output significantly. Oil producing countries were blamed for attempting to rake in larger profits by refusing to increase their production and were labeled as "evil speculators", suspected of manipulating oil rates for higher profit.

But the truth was deeper. They had no spare capacity to produce more. This is the actual limit of what the Earth can give and a real world test for Hubbert's Law.

Many deniers of Peak Oil point to a similar event in recent history (note the sharp dip in the graph around 1975 to 1980) which is the Arab oil embargo of the seventies, when the world was forced to use less oil.

But at that point, there was a political reason for the shortage. It was a political blackmail by the OPEC countries holding the world to ransom. Most people have confused the current inability of oil producers to increase output to be the same kind of political blackmail. This time however, it is a genuine shortage. This is geological Peak Oil and not political.

Proof of Peak Oil in Numbers

The truth about Peak Oil is hiding in plain view in the figures presented by the British Petroleum Statistical Review of World Energy (2011).

The table contains a list of all oil producing countries and regions in the world, along with the production status of each, ordered by year of peak production. The data was originally posted by Praveen Ghanta on *The Oil Drum*, a comprehensive website on discussing Peak Oil. You can find this updated list on Praveen's blog at: *http://truecostblog.com/2012/01/21/ countries-by-peak-oil-date-2011-data-update/*

The table shows that 41 of the 53 oil producing nations in the world have reached Peak Oil production.

This means 78 % of the World's Oil Producing Countries are well past their Peak Production and in steep decline.

Production numbers are quoted in thousands of barrels/day.

Take note of the figures in red in the % Off Peak column.

Country	Peak Prod.	2010 Prod	% Off Peak	Peak Year
US	11297	7513	-33.50%	1970
VENEZUELA	3754	2471	-34.20%	1970
OTHER MIDDLE EAST	79	38	-52.20%	1970
LIBYA	3357	1659	-50.60%	1970
KUWAIT	3339	2508	-24.90%	1972
IRAN	6060	4245	-30.00%	1974
ROMANIA	313	89	-71.50%	1976
INDONESIA	1685	986	-41.50%	1977
TRINIDAD & TOBAGO	230	146	-36.60%	1978
IRAQ	3489	2460	-29.50%	1979?
BRUNEI	261	172	-34.00%	1979
PERU	196	157	-19.80%	1980
TUNISIA	118	80	-32.70%	1980
OTHER EUROPE & EURASIA	12938	374	-97.10%	1983
OTHER AFRICA	241	143	-41.00%	1985
RUSSIAN FEDERATION	11484	10270	-10.60%	1987
EGYPT	941	736	-21.70%	1993
SYRIA	596	385	-35.40%	1995
GABON	365	245	-32.80%	1996
ARGENTINA	890	651	-26.90%	1998
UZBEKISTAN	191	87	-54.50%	1998
COLOMBIA	838	801	-4.50%	1999?
UNITED KINGDOM	2909	1339	-54.00%	1999
AUSTRALIA	809	562	-30.50%	2000
NORWAY	3418	2137	-37.50%	2001
OMAN	960	865	-9.90%	2001?
YEMEN	457	264	-42.20%	2002
OTHER S. & CENT. AMERICA	153	131	-14.20%	2003
MEXICO	3824	2958	-22.60%	2004
DENMARK	390	249	-36.00%	2004
MALAYSIA	793	716	-9.70%	2004?
VIETNAM	427	370	-13.50%	2004
ITALY	127	106	-16.40%	2005
SAUDI ARABIA	11114	10007	-10.00%	2005?
CHAD	173	122	-29.70%	2005

Country	Peak Prod.	2010 Prod	% Off Peak	Peak Year
EQUATORIAL GUINEA	358	274	*-23.50%*	2005
NIGERIA	2499	2402	*-3.90%*	2005?
ECUADOR	545	495	*-9.10%*	2006?
UNITED ARAB EMIRATES	3149	2849	*-9.50%*	2006?
ALGERIA	2016	1809	*-10.20%*	2007
ANGOLA	1875	1851	*-1.30%*	2008 / Growing
OTHER ASIA PACIFIC	340	312	*-8.20%*	2008?
CANADA	3336	3336	-	Growing
BRAZIL	2137	2137	-	Growing
AZERBAIJAN	1037	1037	-	Growing
KAZAKHSTAN	1757	1757	-	Growing
TURKMENISTAN	216	216	-	Growing
QATAR	1569	1569	-	Growing
REP. OF CONGO (BRAZZAVILLE)	292	292	-	Growing
SUDAN	486	486	-	Growing
CHINA	4071	4071	-	Growing
INDIA	826	826	-	Growing
THAILAND	334	334	-	Growing
Peaked /Flat Countries Total		64,182		*78.2% of world oil production*
Growing Countries Total		17,912		*21.8% of world oil production*

With official industry figures like these, the evidence of the demise of the cheap oil era has become insurmountable. In the face of the highest oil prices on record in 2008, the great majority of the world's oil producers were incapable of taking advantage and producing more oil.

This list shows that the world is relying on a small number of countries to keep providing cheap oil. Many nations, including the U.S., saw their oil production peak decades ago. There simply is no turning the clock back.

How much Oil is Left?

Only a few countries belonging to the Organization of the Petroleum Exporting Countries (OPEC) can actually increase oil production effectively. And the world is heavily relying on that.

So obviously the big concern should be how much oil does OPEC say they have left? Given that the OPEC tends to be extremely covert regarding their oil data, we should be asking ourselves "How accurate, or how honest, are their reserve figures?".

Colin J. Campbell, PhD Oxford, is a retired British petroleum geologist who predicted that oil production would peak by 2007. He has pointed to numerous discrepancies in estimates regarding Middle East reserves. The extent of reserves reported by each country remained amazingly constant from year to year and then jumped dramatically. The amazing thing is that the unexplainable surge occurred sometimes even in the total absence of exploration, strongly suggesting that OPEC's reserves are overstated.

Year	Abu Dhabi	Dubai	Iran	Iraq	Kuwait	Neutral zone	Saudi Arabia	Venezuela
1980	28.0	1.4	58.0	31.0	65.4	6.1	163.4	17.9
1981	29.0	1.4	57.5	30.0	65.9	6.0	165.0	18.0
1982	30.6	1.3	57.0	29.7	64.5	5.9	164.6	20.3
1983	30.5	1.4	55.3	**41.0**	64.2	5.7	162.4	21.5
1984	30.4	1.4	51.0	43.0	63.9	5.6	166.0	24.9
1985	30.5	1.4	48.5	44.5	**90.0**	5.4	169.0	25.9
1986	30.0	1.4	47.9	44.1	89.8	5.4	168.8	25.6
1987	31.0	1.4	48.8	47.1	91.9	5.3	166.6	25.0
1988	**92.2**	**4.0**	**92.9**	**100.0**	91.9	5.2	167.0	**56.3**
1989	92.2	4.0	92.9	100.0	91.9	5.2	170.0	58.1
1990	92.2	4.0	92.9	100.0	91.9	5.0	**257.5**	59.1
1991	92.2	4.0	92.9	100.0	94.5	5.0	257.5	59.1
1992	92.2	4.0	92.9	100.0	94.0	5.0	257.9	62.7
1993	92.2	4.0	92.9	100.0	94.0	5.0	258.7	63.3
1994	92.2	4.0	89.3	100.0	94.0	5.0	258.7	64.5
1995	92.2	4.0	88.2	100.0	94.0	5.0	258.7	64.9
1996	92.2	4.0	93.0	112.0	94.0	5.0	259.0	64.9
1997	92.2	4.0	93.0	112.5	94.0	5.0	259.0	71.7
1998	92.2	4.0	89.7	112.5	94.0	5.0	259.0	72.6
1999	92.2	4.0	89.7	112.5	94.0	5.0	261.0	72.6

The chart on the previous page is a chart of the history of reserves for each country (in Billions of Barrels of Oil). The yellow highlighted figures are the sudden unaccounted jumps in reserve figures.

Iraq started the trend in 1983 to be followed by Kuwait in 1985. In 1988, Abu Dhabi, Dubai, Iran, Iraq and Venezuela reported an increase of oil reserves by a factor of 2 to 3 times. Saudi Arabia followed suit 2 years later in 1990 and doubled its reserves from 170 billion barrels to 257.5 billion barrels! That is simply amazing, as a quick review of their prevailing history tells a different story.

This strange phenomenon is easily understood when we probe a little deeper.

Earlier, each OPEC nation was assigned a share of the oil market based on the country's annual **production** capacity. In other words the more the production capacity of an OPEC country, the higher the quota of oil it was allowed to sell in the market.

OPEC changed the rule in the 1980s to allot quota based not only on production capacity, but also on the oil **reserves** that the country claimed it had discovered below the ground.

Now, you can imagine what happens if each country in this cartel, called OPEC, wants to gain an edge over its other members and be allowed to sell more oil. Simple. Each country just claims that they have found more oil!

And sure enough, in the late 1980s there were huge and abrupt increases in the announced oil reserves for several OPEC nations. Obviously, it was in their interest to suddenly report amazing new finds of oil simply so each could sell a greater quota of oil as per the rules stated above.

The World through the Lens of Peak Oil

The last 100 years of industrial reality have conditioned us to look at the world in a particular way. We expect things to become faster, cheaper and more convenient. And we assume this will happen for ever. We look at life through this lens and therefore do not recognize world events for what they really represent. For instance, the world is certainly aware that something economically painful is happening all over. The relentless consistency of financial failures has stumped the best of minds.

- Food prices and living expenses shooting up globally.

- Social unrest erupting in various parts of the world.

- Real estate prices crashing in the U.S.

- Global Financial Collapse of an unprecedented order in 2008 and the persistent recession.

- Mayhem in the Euro zone economies with no end in sight.

- Conventional economic measures such as lowered interest rates, bailouts, quantitative easing and even unabashed money printing consistently failing to stem the financial crisis over the last 5 years.

Yet mainstream news narratives are blaming these events on secondary factors, such as faulty political decisions, misplaced economic policies, manipulation by vested interests and even unfair trade practices in certain countries. Sadly they are clueless about the real underlying causes because our cultural lens of progress and development based on the assumption of infinite resources and energy has trained us to see things in a certain way. And that seemed to work so far because we were on the up-curve of energy, giving us the illusion that it would always hold true. But reaching Peak Oil has inverted the rules of Economics and the way things work.

We now have to see the world through a new lens – the lens of Peak Oil. Only when you take a look through this lens do the dots between these events connect to reveal the truth behind their cause.

Let us examine some of these events a bit closer.

High Food Prices

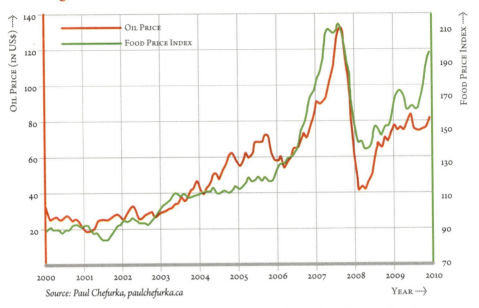

Source: Paul Chefurka, paulchefurka.ca

Industrial food products today completely depend on cheap oil and oil byproducts such as pesticides, herbicides , fertilizers, etc. Both the transportation and the energy used in farming directly depend upon the price of oil.

Therefore oil prices invariably affect the food production industry due to its intensive energy consumption. Today's food prices reflect even the smallest variation in oil prices.

Moreover, the cheap price of oil has allowed extensive industrial agriculture to develop and therefore the prices of food to remain artificially low. As cheap oil runs dry, artificially cheap food will do so too. High food prices are therefore a sure indicator that we have reached Peak Oil.

U.S. Housing Collapse

"I can calculate the movement of the stars, but not the madness of men".

Sir Isaac Newton, after losing a fortune in the South Sea bubble

It all started in the U.S. of A. where they had the smartest and most enterprising financial heads to dream up new ways to try and power the demands of the money curve.

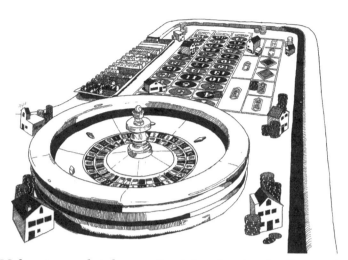

The U.S. housing market degenerating into sub-prime lending was just another way of perpetuating false growth or rather growth beyond the limits that the system was naturally allowing. Remember loaning money at compounding interest rates is the prime mode of money growth. Therefore widening the loan circle to citizens who were clearly not loan-worthy was the first step.

The more a person owed, the more money the banks would make. Therefore, housing debt became a commodity that banks started packaging and selling. This said, there is only so many loan agreements you can issue out.

So Wall Street banks, not content with just that, decided to further leverage their profits. If you remember, leveraging was one of the Concept layers in the **Money Onion** that was mentioned in the first chapter.

So in this case, leveraging meant using mathematical modeling by which banks managed to create sophisticated financial instruments (securitized debt) based on housing mortgages that were essentially limitless in scope.

So while the number of mortgages did not increase, the debt they represented skyrocketed, which is equivalent to the banks printing money. Sadly, the banks made a false assumption that real estate prices would always rise and so imagined that the risks in the bad loans were always covered. Under the stress of high oil prices, rising prices and loss of jobs etc., housing was no longer a priority, leading to a fall in housing prices. The whole scheme back-fired.

The irony is that in hindsight the financial disaster has not even been attributed to the world having reached Peak Oil.

Euro Crisis and World Recession

Then came the Euro debt crisis, which is still foxing the world's best brains. The European Union leaders are unwilling to look the beast in the eye. Debts are toxic and need to be written off since growth is no longer possible and consequently, loans cannot be repaid.

To a casual observer, it may appear as if there is nothing in common between the U.S. housing collapse and the Euro crisis. But in concept, they are fundamentally the same. The only difference is that while in the U.S. the banks schemed to draw new homeowners to take loans that they could not afford, in the Euro zone the trick was finding new countries to extend loans to.

You see, big banks in Europe were limited by the slow-growing, mature economies they operated in. You can't make money if you can't lend it, so they were stymied. The solution was the Eurozone, which expanded boundaries to cover the cash-starved countries of Southern Europe. Banks began lending on the basis that the loans would all be made good by the European Central Bank even if the southerners couldn't pay them back.

This was exactly like Wall Street giving housing mortgages to poor families in the U.S. even though there was no hope of them paying them back. So in Europe it is Greece, Spain, Italy and Portugal who are the poor, about to default on their inflated debt.

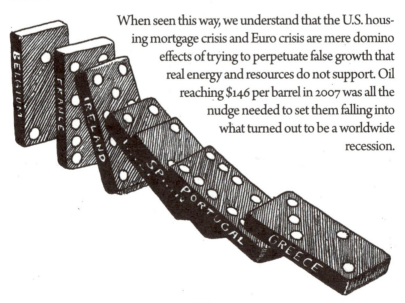

When seen this way, we understand that the U.S. housing mortgage crisis and Euro crisis are mere domino effects of trying to perpetuate false growth that real energy and resources do not support. Oil reaching $146 per barrel in 2007 was all the nudge needed to set them falling into what turned out to be a worldwide recession.

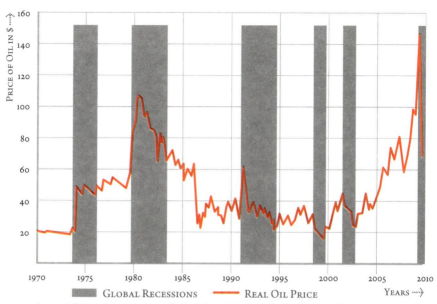

Source: Jeff Rubin & Peter Buchanan, "What's the Real Cause of the Global Recession?", StrategEcon,
Oct. 31, 2008, CIBC World Markets Inc., and Bloomberg.

To further substantiate this argument, let us do a quick review of the correlation between oil price spikes and recessions over the past 50 years.

Five out of six sharp oil spikes resulted in a recession.

This shows us the extent to which oil is a key factor in our financial
stability.

Economists, the business community and world leaders dazed by the
financial collapse are still in severe denial but day by day, the correlation
of high oil prices and financial instability are becoming evident.

Yet, mainstream media avoids the term "Peak Oil" like the plague.

Arab Spring – Unrest in the Middle East

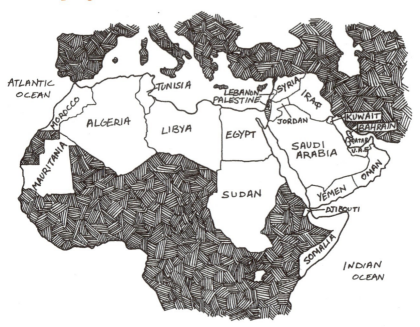

The social unrest that we have been noticing in the Middle East is often perceived as an uprising against an autocratic regime.

And in some countries it is misunderstood as a sectarian clash between Shias and Sunnis.

These are secondary effects. The root cause is the high cost of food and lack of jobs and livelihoods due to high energy prices.

If this sudden spate of unrest were because of the nature of governments, the people would not have tolerated the same regimes for the last 70 or 80 years. Yes, all was fine while the people's fundamental needs of jobs, food and basic necessities were met. There was no need to revolt. Coming down to the streets and facing bullets is not people's first choice. This is the last stage of a system in economic collapse. And that through the lens of Peak Oil is clearly understood as the ripple effect of high energy prices.

Occupy Wall Street

Occupy Wall Street started on September 17, 2011 in the financial district of New York City.

The main issues were social and economic inequality, greed, corruption and the undue influence of corporations on the government.

So the net signal that came through from their protest slogans was that it was all about corporate greed and government connivance. Though these may be valid points for the protest movement, they are not its underlying cause.

Check out this line of causation.

- Much lower real production in the U.S. translates into very small real growth.

- Very small real growth means devising means to fake larger growth.

- Faking growth leads to eventual correction and then financial collapse.

- Financial collapse causes financial crisis.

- Financial crisis means ordinary people lose jobs.

- BUT big banks and big players always get bailed out by the government in a crisis.

- The price tag for the bailout is diverted to the tax-payer who is already jobless.

- For a while the tax-payers don't mind as long as the system can bounce back.

- Peak oil ensures that the system cannot bounce back as growth is geologically not possible.

- Prices soar, job losses soar, production falls further.

- Play it from the top a few times and…

…we get Occupy Wall Street.

Yes, the core driving force is the worldwide shrinkage of economic activity due to a global energy decline. That is Peak Oil.

The tragedy is that most of the poor protestors had no clue of the role of Peak Oil in their lives. Which is why their anger and revolt seemed misguided against the corporates who are themselves victims of an End of Growth scenario brought on by Peak Oil.

Nothing Seems to Work

This brings us to the last sign: no amount of corrective economic and political measures seems to be working. And that is because nothing can kick-start growth if the very basis of growth is to run a system that was built on the premise of infinite supplies of cheap energy. And it is not as though the world's energy supplies are suddenly over. It is only that we are entering the downside of the curve – Hubbert's Curve – that tells the plain truth of how we get energy and resources from the Earth.

Yes, bailout of the institutions and big banks could have helped if their mistake was a genuine error of judgment and not a deliberate effort to redefine a financial system along the lines of gambling and financial jugglery.

Yes, we could have generated more credit in the circular fashion, as we always did, if it was possible to produce more goods to service that credit. But goods need real resources and cheap energy to be in fact "good".

Yes, we could have lowered interest rates to encourage enterprises to take loans if taking those loans could somehow result in entrepreneurs coming up with new products that could actually be sold at a profit. But in a large part of the western world, the interest rates are already near zero and most people are opting for "needs" over "wants".

Yes, quantitative easing could have helped lubricate financial pipelines if the problem was only a congestion of financial arteries.

So, because nothing is working at this point of time, it is a scenario of "no holds barred".

Big money is doing what it can to protect its interest even if it means being in bed with the government. They are getting bailouts which the general public will have to pay with taxes over the next several generations.

The government is going through the moves of betting future public money, in the form of bailouts and quantitative easing, on schemes that it well knows will fail.

The irony is that the public is keeping its mouth shut because it somehow wants the system to work and does not know any other way to get out of this mess.

And the mess is that we are unwilling to believe that maybe, just maybe, growth is over. The tide has turned. The peak has been reached.

Peak Oil Denial

Even where the impacts of Peak Oil are glaring and self-evident, the pitch of denial gets shriller.

First of all, let us ask the question: Why is there is so much denial and opposition to Peak Oil even in the face of such concrete and damning data? And even more, why is the sharpest denial coming from people who should be well aware of the exact position of oil reserves and depletion data – such as oil companies, government agencies, energy and resource organizations and the media?

The answer is that if they admit to the reality of Peak Oil, then they are also admitting to the end of Quantitative Financial Growth.

This is like a bullet through the head for the Economic Paradigm that we have been following since the invention of money. The very premise of Classical Economics fails.

Not only does it fail, but at this point there is a huge correction of false asset values that has built up in our account books and is just waiting to be reset. That is what they are all petrified about. By denying Peak Oil, its deniers are simply trying to extend the date of inevitable corrections. Nothing more. The only problem is that the longer we all deny Peak Oil and go on with the business of Exponential Growth as usual, the harder and bigger the financial correction will be.

We witnessed one such correction in the 2008 Financial Collapse. That and that alone made a big difference in the stance of those denying Peak Oil. Yet they refuse to use the term "Peak Oil" and evasively call it just about anything else. They called it a "short-term production constraint" or a "tightening of oil supplies". But they will not use the term "Peak Oil" because it contains the word "Peak" and using "Peak" innately concedes the understanding of a one-way decline of oil in the future, meaning the End of Growth!

The Slow Breakdown of Denial

Reality is beginning to make its presence felt. And since 2005 we have had a series of admissions, open and covert, from across the fence. Here I list some in chronological order.

PROOF #1: The Hirsch Report – U.S. Dept. of Energy – Feb 2005

The Hirsch Report, officially called *Peaking of World Oil Production: Impacts, Mitigation, and Risk Management*, was created on request by the U.S. government for the U.S. Department of Energy and was published in February 2005. It is the first official document to take Peak Oil seriously, though at the time of it being commissioned, the government and the person heading the report, Robert Hirsch, were both unprepared for what they were going to uncover. Here is Robert Hirsch in his own words later.

> *"This problem is truly frightening. This problem is like nothing that I have ever seen in my lifetime, and the more you think about it and the more you look at the numbers, the more uneasy any observer gets. [...] And the risks to our economies and our civilization are enormous."* [1]

Now that is a fairly candid bit of acknowledgment of Peak Oil. You can read the Hirsch Report at *http://dspace.library.cornell.edu/handle/1813/692*

PROOF #2: International Energy Agency (I.E.A.) - 2007

This report estimates that the world's existing oilfields would decline at around 3.7% per annum.

By 2008, the same agency doubled the forecast decline rate to 6.7% per annum.

Check page 84 of the 2007 report or page 45 of the 2008 report which you can find at the following links:

http://www.worldenergyoutlook.org/media/weawebsite/2008-1994/weo2007.pdf

http://www.worldenergyoutlook.org/media/weowebsite/2008-1994/weo2008.pdf

PROOF #3: U.S. Military Report – Sept 2010

The U.S. military is well aware of the problem. The 2010 Joint Operating Environment Report stated:

> "By 2012, surplus oil production capacity could entirely disappear, and as early as 2015, the shortfall in output could reach nearly 10 million barrels per day".

You can find the details on page 29 of this document at: *http://www.fas.org/man/eprint/joe2010.pdf*

PROOF #4: Big Oil Companies Admit to Peak Oil

The world's most important oil companies have always been opposed to the concept of peak oil and have insisted in reassuring the general public that there would be no oil deficit in sight until 2050.

The increasing evidence was however too obvious, and even though the companies started admitting to shortages they were careful to avoid the word "Peak". Ron Oxburgh, who is the former chairman of Shell, has said:

> "It is pretty clear that there is not much chance of finding any significant quantity of new cheap oil. Any new or unconventional oil is going to be expensive". [2]

Exxon is one of the world's richest oil companies. Its official spokesman admitted:

> "All the easy oil and gas in the world has pretty much been found. Now comes the harder work in finding and producing oil from more challenging environments and work areas". [3]

PROOF #5: OPEC Fails to Increase Output

In 2007, when oil prices were escalating and spare oil production capacity was sorely needed, the world pleaded and urged the OPEC to increase its oil production so that oil rates would stop rising uncontrollably. OPEC was unable to increase its oil output in spite of repeated attempts to reassure, until oil reached an unprecedented high of 146 dollars/barrel.

OPEC claimed that the issue was solely a supply shortage that could be countered through investment and technology solutions. The word "peak" was carefully avoided, as it would have equaled to admitting that Hubbert's Law was a true threat that could apply to the powerful OPEC.

Summing up Peak Oil Denial

Honestly, whether any of these folks actually use the term "Peak Oil" or not is irrelevant, as we are presently experiencing the effects of what a peak of energy would feel like.

Each and every statistic points to the fact that we are well beyond the peak. The math of geology is well defined and we can no longer brush off the facts.

Therefore, I do not wish to labor a point that is already evident. What is more important and urgent is to examine what our responses for the future should be in the face of Peak Oil.

The next section is about evaluating the options of dealing with Peak Oil.

Welcome to the slippery world of Alternative Energy Solutions.

Part III

Alternative Energy Solutions
A Mirage of Hope

There has to be a "Solution"!

The strongest, silent proof of Peak Oil is the energy crunch that is getting worse by the day. No wonder you hear shrill cries for energy "solutions" from all directions. And so there are all kinds of "solutions" being discussed. But in this mad rush for so called "solutions" we are missing something. Let me deviate a bit to clarify the meaning of the word "solution".

John Michael Greer explains the definition of 'solutions' very elegantly on his blog *The Archdruid Report*. He explains that first, it is crucial to understand the difference between a "problem" and a "predicament". Problems have solutions. But predicaments are a nature of reality and we have to cope with them. They do not have solutions. He says:

> "For instance, traffic congestion is a problem and we can find a solution for it: wider roads, by-passes, overhead bridges, etc. But death is a predicament. There is no way to get around it, even if we prolong life expectation.
>
> Therefore Peak Oil is a predicament and not a problem. The finiteness of our planet and the availability of resources are also predicaments, alike the finiteness of an individual's life. Yet somehow, people have mistaken the finiteness of our planet and its resources as a problem."

It is obvious that perpetual, exponential growth is impossible on a finite planet. Therefore the limits set by our planet should be considered as an inevitable predicament, for which we need to figure out coping strategies and not a denial approach.

If we had become aware of this in the '70s, addressing the issue with changes in the way we do business, in our economy and lifestyle, we could still be treating them as a problem for which we can find solutions. Sadly, we have reached Peak Oil without doing anything about it during all this time and the problem has therefore definitely become a predicament.

Now that we acknowledge that we are in a predicament we will understand that most of the solutions offered are false because they are in fact trying to find a way to preserve the crazy paradigm of Perpetual Growth, which is an unsolvable problem.

So to get over this we first need to understand that Perpetual Growth is not possible and we have to start looking at what our responses to the new emerging reality should be rather than search for solutions.

When you mistake a predicament for a problem you only come up with **False Solutions**. And the focus of my argument is to dismantle all the False Solutions being paraded around these days as grand saviors for the energy fix we find ourselves in.

Here are some of the responses I have come across most frequently.

FALSE SOLUTION	FALSE BELIEF
1. Half the Oil is still Left	We have lots of time.
2. Find More Oil	We can, as we have done it in the past!
3. Increase Energy Efficiency	Saving energy will save us.
4. Develop New Technologies	High-tech can achieve anything!
5. Alternative Energy	Other forms of energy can replace oil.
6. Human Ingenuity	Human Intelligence is boundless.

STOP: Before we evaluate each False Solution, let me reiterate that finding any amount of resources or alternatives to feed **Perpetual Exponential Quantitative Growth (PEQG)** is impossible and therefore futile.

That was the whole point of the **Concept** vs. **Reality** argument in the first half of this book.

Our financial **Concept** is INFINITE and the **Reality** on which it is based is FINITE.

Nothing, I repeat nothing, can keep up with exponential growth on a finite planet. Yes, the shocking and dangerous reality is that most of the mainstream energy experts, including most of the alternative energy proponents who ought to be knowing better, are peddling soft lies.

Nothing surprising – a large part of the alternative energy brigade is funded by corporates who are themselves some form of venture capitalists. Their ultimate objective is to sell maximum solar panels or windmills or whatever. They are part of the growth paradigm too. So whatever they say is never going to contest that paradigm ever.

Above that, they are well aware that the general public is waiting to hear some soothing assurances, namely that there will be no energy shortage problems in the future as long as we switch to some alternatives that allow us to run business as usual, which of course means to sustain Perpetual Exponential Quantitative Growth.

This will be evident when we examine False Solutions 1 and 2, which illustrate the futility of battling the exponential. Nevertheless, we will examine each of these False Solutions in detail to fully comprehend the sheer limitations of each of these beliefs.

False Solution # 1: Half the Oil is still Left
FALSE BELIEF: We have lots of time.

The first of the False Solutions is the most natural for people to assume. They wonder why anyone should worry when we have reached ONLY the halfway point of oil reserves. After all no one worries when their petrol tank is half empty. Surely we have a lot of time through the second half of oil reserves to take suitable steps and get out of this mess.

Let us examine an example presented by A. A. Bartlett, Prof. Emeritus of Physics, Univ. of Colorado, Boulder, USA. He illustrates what exactly happens when anything is half-gone in an exponential scenario.

Imagine a glass that is empty at 11 pm at night.

We put one bacteria in it at 11 pm.

The bacteria has the property to double every minute.

It is 60 minutes before midnight.

At **11:01 pm** there are 2 bacteria.

At **11:02 pm** there are 4 bacteria.

At **11:03 pm** there are 8 bacteria. And so on...

At midnight the glass is full of bacteria.

QUESTION:
When was the glass half full?

THE ANSWER:

1 minute before midnight!

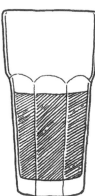

Because the bacteria doubled every minute, half a glass of bacteria became a full glass in just one minute. 1 minute is therefore the **doubling time**.

So it took **59 minutes** for the glass to become half full.

Then, it took just **1 minute** for the second half to fill up.

THAT is the power of exponential growth.

The formula for calculating the doubling time in a compounding growth case is well known to money managers. It is simplified as

Doubling time = 70/Rate of growth

In our economic paradigm of Exponential Growth, if we are experiencing **5%** compound growth annually, the **doubling time** is 70/5, which is just **14 years**.

So if you have consumed half the oil on the planet and insist on 5% annual growth, you have only 1 doubling time, and that is 14 years, to finish the remaining oil!

Taking this example a little further, we realize that just 3 minutes before midnight, i.e. just 3 doubling times earlier, the glass was only 12.5% full.

Would anyone at this point flag a danger signal?

Certainly not! But that again is the danger of an exponential growth paradigm.

How much Oil is Used in each Doubling Time?

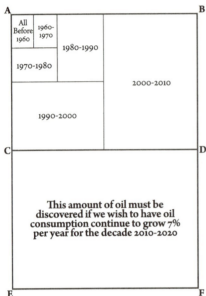

One shocking reality of the doubling paradigm is that in each doubling you use the sum of all the previous doubling times!

Look at the diagram on the left. Start from the smallest rectangle at the top left corner. It represents all the oil produced before 1960.

At 7% growth you double that rectangle for each decade of oil consumption as labelled.

Here you can see how in each doubling time you are using the sum of all the oil upto that date. The bottom rectangle CEFD represents the total oil needed to be discovered between 2010-2020. This is clearly equal to the area of all the preceding rectangles marked as ACDB, which means all the oil used since the discovery of oil upto 2010.

This is another way to illustrate the danger of an exponential growth paradigm.

Of course, if the annual growth rate was less, the doubling time would be longer, but not much longer as we can see from the chart below. In India and China, which is a third of the consumer population, we are insisting on achieving growth rates above 7 to 8 percent.

In this chart we have Growth Rate vs. Doubling Time. And you can see it does not make much difference. It is all within a life span.

Growth Rate(%)	Doubling Time (yrs)
7	10
6	11.67
5	14
4	17.5
3	23.33
2	35

False Solution # 2: Find more Oil

FALSE BELIEF: We can, as we have done it in the past.

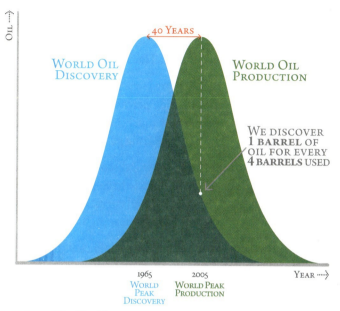

Discovery vs. Production

Ok, so let us for a moment forget all this doubling stuff. That is just mathematics, you might say. We humans constructed mathematics, so surely we can beat it. Let us see if that is possible.

So instead of worrying about reaching the peak, we will simply go and look for more oil. After all, we have done that in the past. So why not now?

The slight hitch is that you have to first discover oil before you can extract and produce it.

So there is obviously some lag time between discovery and production. Hubbert had discovered back then that this lag time was 40 years. Today that gap is shorter because of improved technology but nevertheless there is a gap between discovery and production.

So the **blue curve** of oil discovery is followed by the **green curve** of oil production after a gap of 40 years.

We are today at the top of the green curve, remember, that is the peak of oil production.

115

So how much oil are we discovering today?

Just draw a line down from the top of the **green production** curve to where it meets the **blue discovery** curve. That figure is what we are discovering today. And guess what? We are discovering less than 25% of what we are producing and using today. In other words, we are finding only one barrel for every 4 barrels we are using. Hardly a recipe for sustainability.

Besides that, it is now widely acknowledged by the world's leading petroleum geologists that more than 95 percent of all recoverable oil has already been found. So, there is not much hope of suddenly finding a huge amount of oil. The days of discovering giant oil fields are gone.

Therefore, when we say glibly that we will discover more oil, it sounds a bit fanciful. It would take one giant miracle to suddenly discover enough oil to even equal the level of the production curve. And we would have to do this consistently every year for it to be meaningful.

Oil prices have tripled since 2003. The market logic tells us that if we need to increase our oil output all we need to do is allocate huge amounts of money and capital in oil exploration and the Earth will still pour out bountiful cheap oil like in the golden years. This in fact is the pitch of self-serving companies and misinformed politicians. They need to accept the limits of the Hubberts curve.

Add to this the fact that the exponential use of oil still hangs like a specter over our plans of Perpetual Exponential Growth.

FALSE SOLUTION # 2 (Continued): Find more Oil

But say you are not convinced that we have looked hard enough for new oil or that new technologies will help us find oil in yet unreachable places.

Let us go back to our bacteria in a glass example.

Say that 1 minute before midnight the bacteria miraculously find 3 more empty glasses.

This is equivalent to us finding **6 TRILLION** barrels of oil today, when we feel we have reached Peak Oil.

This is **6 times** the total amount of oil that the world has already consumed since oil was discovered.

Which of course is **6 times** the total amount of remaining known oil reserves.

This is a total and complete fantasy but we will consider it anyway to illustrate the hazards of exponential growth.

So here are the 3 new empty glasses. And the first is half-gone at 1 minute before midnight.

THE QUESTION:

How long do we have before all the glasses are full of bacteria, meaning that all the oil is depleted?

The Answer:

Starting

1 minute later

2 minutes later

3 minutes later

Just 3 minutes, which means 3 doubling times, is all it needs to finish the absolutely unbelievable and preposterous quantity of 7 trillion barrels of oil.

Of those, 1 trillion are real, as we know they exist and 6 trillion are completely imaginary which, incidentally, nobody in any sphere of the oil industry or any geological circle believes we can find or exists.

In our real world context of exponential growth at the rate of 5%, it means that in 42 years the absolutely fantastic find of 7 trillion barrels of oil will be gone!

Finding oil in arithmetic quantities does not help when we are consuming it exponentially.

These illustrations reveal the dangerous nature of exponential growth!

And exponential growth is exactly what we have built into our very concept of economics.

Remember, money must grow by P% every year.

This growth must compound forever!

Sounds great when it is money coming in. But horrifying when it is resources or oil going out.

It is clearly impossible to keep pace with anything that grows exponentially.

Now this should make your ponder the next time someone confidently reassures you that "we can always find more oil".

"The greatest shortcoming of the human race is our inability to understand the exponential function".

A. A. Bartlett - Prof. Emeritus of Physics, University of Colorado, Boulder, U.S.A.

False Solution # 3: Energy Efficiency
FALSE BELIEF: Saving energy will save us.

The next most obvious solution that comes to mind in dealing with the energy crisis is the aspect of Energy Efficiency. Even well informed people are quick to jump to this option without considering the entire scenario of our industrial world. Let us start with a statement of fact and a simple question.

FACT:

It is true that every gadget, device, machine or process in the last 150 years of the industrial age has been more energy efficient than its predecessor.

QUESTION:

Then how come the world's **Gross Energy Consumption** is always increasing as per the graph below?

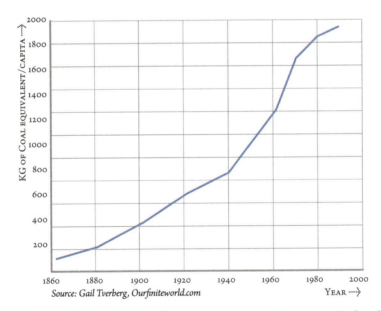

Source: Gail Tverberg, Ourfiniteworld.com

Obviously, efficiency has hardly helped over the last 150 years. In fact the trend is merrily going along the lines of exponential growth as if nothing had been done.

Then why do we cite efficiency as the way to get out of the energy crisis?

Maybe we need to take a much closer look at what this means. It is not so obvious on the face of it.

Jevon's Paradox

In 1865, the English economist William Stanley Jevons, observed that technological improvements that increased the efficiency of coal use led to the increased consumption of coal in a wide range of industries. He argued that, contrary to common intuition, technological improvements in fact resulted in an increase in fuel consumption.

This observation was first stated as a paradox. But I will explain why it is not really a paradox but something to be expected in the way we have chosen to run our modern industrial world.

One way to understand this is that greater efficiency in the use of a resource has historically resulted in a lower price per unit for the purchaser. If the cost is lower, the product becomes more affordable to more purchasers, and use tends to increase, not decrease. This, I call the "proliferation effect".

Another way of explaining this apparent paradox is that all industries who manufacture or use energy-saving devices or services are eventually part of an Exponential Economic Growth paradigm. So they will try to grow no matter what. If any industry invents an energy-saving device it merely uses that advantage to produce more goods to generate more profits, and that negates any saving of gross energy consumed.

The economic world that we live in is similar to a huge expanding box.

What we do inside the box makes really no difference because eventually the rules are that the box has to expand – money has to grow with time. That is the governing rule of Perpetual Exponential Economic Growth.

So you see, it is not really a paradox at all, as Mr. Jevon called it, but something to be expected. There is no escape in a perpetual growth syndrome.

Many people who are attempting to save energy or use energy-efficient devices may get upset with this line of thinking . They may feel that this line of reasoning is discouraging to anyone attempting to save energy.

That is not the case I am making. I am simply saying that we first have to change the rules and stop the "box" from growing exponentially. One must first examine the **Concept** of Exponential Growth that governs all economics, industry and resource and energy usage. That is what finally defines gross energy used (as per the graph shown above). And therefore gross energy used cannot be offset by individual energy saving devices or processes because they are eventually used to propagate growth.

You first have to address the PEQG paradigm and say goodbye to the concept of perpetual growth and only then will your efforts of using energy-saving devices and energy-saving habits show effect.

Change your Lens

I will now illustrate the energy saving illusion with a specific example of an energy-saving device. I will show that the illusion is due to our wrong perspective. Are we using a close-up lens or a wide-angle lens to evaluate energy usage? Let me illustrate.

For example, when electronics first came about, there were these huge, bulky, glowing devices called valves that were used in making radios, amplifiers, transmitters and all kinds of electronics.

They were in fact, like an incandescent bulb that heated a filament and a lot of energy was wasted in the form of heat.

They were also very bulky and clearly required a fair bit of glass and metal to manufacture.

Then around the early '50s came an earth-shaking new electronic device based on a completely different technology called semiconductors. It was called a transistor and it used a millionth of the power compared to a vacuum tube.

It was also much smaller and cheaper per piece.

Now here comes the lens of our perspective.

If you look through a close-up lens at ONLY one transistor, then it uses a millionth of the energy of a vacuum tube. It appears as if energy is saved by a factor of millions.

BUT if you were to use a wider lens and examine how the total electronic industry exploded due to the invention of the transistor, then the answer is dramatically different. While the world had earlier manufactured vacuum tubes in millions, we now produced transistors in hundreds of billions!

Now if you added up all the energy that was being used to manufacture transistors and add to it all the energy used by them, you would realize that their invention resulted in the world using a lot more energy.

Time to learn an energy principle: Besides that simple escalation of numbers, there is another hidden aspect to energy used in high-tech devices called **Embedded Energy.**

A lot more energy goes into manufacturing transistors, as they require a lot more precise engineering, purification of materials, precise machines to assemble, dust-controlled atmosphere, sophisticated factories, highly trained staff, etc. If you examine the complete infrastructure that manufactures all these transistors, do a summation of the energy that is put in and then divide it by the number of transistors being manufactured, you will realize that each transistor carries a great amount of **embedded energy**, and that too offsets the energy that the transistor actually saves.

Conclusion: Energy efficiency can never help save energy in a growth and high-tech paradigm. Yes, in the next section (False solution #4) on Technology we will see how immensely energy-dependent technology really is.

The Boat with an Exponential Hole

Probably the simplest real life analogy to illustrate the futility of energy-efficiency in a Growth Paradigm is through a situation I call the "Boat with the Exponential Hole".

Imagine that you are on a boat and it springs a very small hole below the waterline and water starts gushing in.

As parts around the hole are steadily giving way, the hole gets larger, so a few of the passengers rush around finding whatever they can to empty the water manually.

For a while it seems to work, but soon it becomes clear that in fact the hole is doubling at regular intervals. The passengers are doing whatever they can to keep pace.

The passengers manage to overcome several doublings of the hole till they reach their maximum speed of bailing. It is evident now that they are doomed once the next doubling of the hole happens.

Did you notice that while everything was being done to bail the water out, nothing was being done to plug or repair the hole – to stop it from doubling? If the folk on the boat would have turned their attention to fixing the hole, it would stop growing exponentially. Then with more work done on it, the hole would also stop growing and become of a fixed size. That itself would make the bailing exercise viable.

So if you eventually want to stop bailing you have to plug the hole. Simple!

In our industrial world, the expanding hole represents the concept of exponential growth and the bailing out of water represents our measures of energy efficiency and energy saving. One is exponential and the other is arithmetic. The remedial measures cannot rise exponentially but the economic market/energy consumption is growing exponentially. So the two scales just do not compare.

So when will we stop seeking escape in the illusion that "Energy Efficiency and Energy Saving will save us"?

Let us get real in understanding and addressing the root cause of our predicament: our economic paradigm of Exponential Growth.

False Solution # 4: Technology
FALSE BELIEF: High-tech can achieve anything.

Technology is revered as a kind of supernatural force. There seems to be an almost blind faith in what it can achieve. And so in the closing rounds of any discussion on energy depletion, we hear calls to this faith with the hypnotic mantra "Technology will find a way".

Undoubtedly, there is a reason for this belief. Because in the past it appeared as if technology did indeed find us a way to achieve so many mind-blowing things to our advantage. But that is when we had plenty of energy and we will soon see that technology is governed by the basic laws of physics and thermodynamics. Much of our existing technology simply won't work without an abundant underlying fossil fuel base.

There are 2 ways in which people are expecting technology to help us in the oil depletion scenario.

1. By improved methods of extracting oil, coal, natural gas and other conventional energy resources.

2. By discovering a completely new kind of energy source.

Regarding the first point, it is important to understand that improved technology can at best work to postpone the arrival of Peak Oil or peak of any resource. It cannot however make the peak go away.

As for the second point of finding new technologies, so far that has proved to be a mirage. All our current ideas of technology energy fixes consist of shuffling energy from one form to another with the downside of energy loss in each conversion.

There is nothing on the horizon that is even remotely promising to generate surplus, clean energy without oil dependency. We go in great detail on this in the next section on **Alternative Energies**.

But for our better understanding, let us first unravel what exactly is technology.

What is Technology?

Technology is usually confused with a tool. Most often, we interchange the word "technology" and "tool" in our mind without realizing it. We imagine that just as we buy a tool and it is then there for us to use at any time, so is it with technology. That once we have come up with a particular kind of technology, it is there to stay with us forever.

This is completely untrue as they are two completely different entities. Let us go through the steps – by starting with tools and ending with technology.

All living creatures manipulate their environment to suit their purpose. A bird will build a nest with its beak. A beaver will use its teeth to chew branches and then place them to build a dam, etc. Humans too manipulate their environment to suit their purpose.

The simplest way for us humans to manipulate our environment is with a tool.

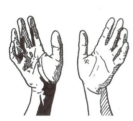

The first human tools really are our hands. That is how we physically manipulate our environment to suit our purpose.

But the beauty of our hands is that they are always there at our service and they require very little energy and resources apart from our normal diet to operate and maintain.

A step up is a **manual tool** like a hammer, screwdriver, saw, garden hoe, pitch-fork, etc.

They increase the ability of humans to manipulate our environment.

But it takes a certain amount of resources and energy to make these manual tools. However once manufactured, they do not need further energy or resources to maintain or run them.

Next step up is an **automated tool** like an electric drill, lathe, electric saw, etc.

They allow an even greater manipulation of our environment but are more vulnerable to needs

127

of energy, resources, special fuels to build and maintain them and to ensure that they operate smoothly.

They also require more knowledge and training to operate and maintain. Above all, they require a source of energy to run them.

Going up the ladder, we come to the **machine**.

This is a complex collection of parts that requires significantly more energy to design, build, maintain and operate.

It also requires specialized knowledge to design, build, maintain and operate. And machines need a lot more energy for their maintenance and in order to run properly.

So a machine is even more vulnerable, as many more specific things are needed to make machines possible. The complexity is increasing and complexity always comes at an energy cost.

And finally we step up to something called a **technology**.

A technology is a "coming together" of all of the above and a lot more that makes that particular kind of technology possible and affordable at that point of time.

A technology is a wide-spread and complex network of innumerable factors working together. Intangible really and hard to completely get your mind around. Here is why.

Technology is a coming-together of:

Ideas
Designs
Raw materials
Processes
Special tools
Special machines
Special skills
Trained labor
Economic viabilities
Government policies
Transport networks
and many more...

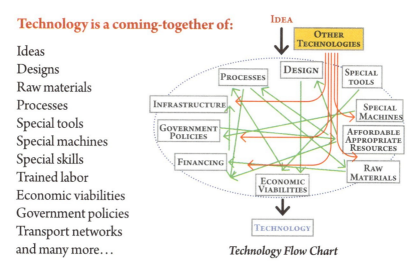

Technology Flow Chart

All these inputs are interlinked in complex ways often difficult to trace and very often depend on other technologies which are themselves dependent on other technologies. And this mind-boggling interconnected web of dependency is obviously held together with a whole lot of cheap energy and resources.

So for a start, any crisis in energy is sure to hit technology hard.

So you see that any technology is immensely vulnerable to the slightest change in any of the many inputs. You remove one of them and that technology can fail instantly unless you quickly find a replacement and that too at the right cost etc. The more complex the technology is, the more vulnerable and exposed it is to external factors beyond anyone's control.

Keep that in mind the next time you hear the mantras "Technology will find a Solution" or "High-tech will save the day". What technology worshippers fail to recognize, is that technology, especially high-tech by its very nature, is so dependent on energy (apart from thousands of other inputs that also require energy) that it will be the first thing to collapse in an energy depleting world.

Sad bottom line:

- Technology does not create energy.
- In fact, cheap energy makes technology possible.
- The more energy available – the more high-tech becomes possible.
- Remove that level of availability of energy and resources and "BOOM", that technology is unviable and ceases to exist.

So it is hardly likely that technology will save us!

False Solution # 5: Alternative Energies
FALSE BELIEF: Other forms of energy can replace oil.

> *"Contrary to public perception, renewable energy is not the silver bullet that will solve all our problems".*

Jeroen van der Veer, Former Shell CEO, *The Standard*,
"Three Hard Truths about the World's Energy Crisis"

The word "alternative" says it all. It seems to hold a magic promise. It intrinsically reassures us that the energy is somewhere out there to replace oil and we simply have to get it.

Likewise, don't you wish there were "alternative" jobs for all those who have been laid-off recently around the world?

Then why are they still laid-off? You may say the laid-off folk are simply not trying hard enough to find those "alternative" jobs.

Or maybe the truth is closer to the fact that "alternative" jobs are not paying at the same scale.

What if the new job offered a salary of Rs 60,000 instead of Rs 100,000 and it involves working all night in a seedy part of town with no air-conditioning and fewer holidays… and no free coffee?

So the job-hunter decides to say "no thanks" to that job and just keeps looking.

That is the same story with oil and alternative energies.

Of course there are alternative energies. But how much do they pay-off compared to oil? And what are the other downsides of producing them?

Maybe a hint lies in the fact that we have been talking alternatives for over 4 decades now. Yet alternative energies account for only about 13% of world energy usage, despite generous subsidies by governments all over.

Or maybe the truth is that most alternatives are all like the low paying jobs. They all offer less and therefore will not run our high energy dependent modern world or business as usual. The net energy they provide is either less or marginal compared to the energy you put in (mostly oil energy).

That is like taking up a new 60k job but still needing the old 100k job to keep your life on an even keel. I don't think that your ex-boss had that in mind when he gave you the slip.

So while we can hold on to oil for a bit longer to run our "alternative" plans, we have to be careful because we must not squander the remaining valuable oil on our experiments with alternatives. At some point, the alternatives should better be able to stand on their own without the help of too much oil. Preferably none.

And more importantly, the alternative energy "solutions" had better return us more energy than we are putting in to make and maintain them. Or there is no point investing in them. Right?

This is a fundamental energy principle and it is called Energy Returned on Energy Invested (ERoEI) or Net Energy. It is kind of how your business-sale price has to be greater than cost price to have a net positive profit.

So that brings us to **ENERGY RULE #1 - NET ENERGY (ERoEI): The Net Energy gained has to be suitably high for an alternative to be viable.**

Some alternatives like solar and wind energy can have a reasonably high Net Energy return. But then the next factor is cost.

In present times, it has become evident that none of the alternatives can compete with oil on cost.

So alternative energy experts advise us to wait for oil prices to go up for the good old market wisdom to apply. Namely that when the price of oil gets high enough, the alternatives will become worth it and the market will find a way to replace oil.

But I thought the markets were down exactly for the reason that oil prices were too high. And they are not showing signs of going anywhere near the old levels. Remember? Oil is on the downslope of old Hubbert's curve. Which means it will only get more expensive.

Wait a minute! I feel like I am watching my dog chasing its tail.

- Alternatives are expensive in relation to oil.
- Just wait for oil to go up, then alternatives will be worth it.
- Oil goes up and alternatives get more expensive.
- Just wait a little longer for oil to go up again.
- Oil goes up… alternatives get more expensive.

Round and round and round we go.

My head is spinning. Please stop.

What am I missing?

Well for a start that the tail is attached to the end of the same dog that is turning.

Alternatives are the tail. They are ALL made with oil energy and byproducts. And anyone who does not tell you that, is covering a big fat lie. No matter how fancy their alternative energy "solution" is.

Solar, Wind, Hydro, Nuclear, Bio-fuels, Tar sands, Oil shale, Hydrogen, Fuel cells – you name it and they are ALL built, run, maintained and then replaced on an oil based infrastructure. They all take a lot of energy to construct and require a petroleum platform to work off. They are not in that sense an alternative at all!

I would call them energy converters. Put in oil energy to make solar panels, windmills, nuclear plants and out comes electrical energy at great cost.

They are all like your 60k job that needs your 100k job to maintain your lifestyle.

And that is where we are stuck.

This brings us **ENERGY RULE #2 - OIL DEPENDENCY: the alternative must not be too dependant on oil and its price.**

Well apart from Net Energy and Oil Dependency, alternatives fail at another fundamental level. Most of them are dilute energies. This is because they extract energy as it arrives in real time. Solar, wind, bio-fuels, bio-mass, wave, tidal, geothermal, etc. involve collecting or extracting energy as it arrives from sunlight, wind, plant growth or heat from the Earth.

Because this is in real time, it is dilute energy compared to fossil fuels – especially oil.

In contrast, fossil fuels allow us to tap the energy of millions of years of stored sunlight at once. Therefore, fossil fuels are an immensely dense form of energy.

To illustrate this point, let us compare the flow of water from rain as opposed to from a reservoir.

Alternative Energies are like the rain.

It is water falling in real time.

The flow is dilute – distributed over a large area and time.

It needs to be collected to be useful.

Fossil fuels are like the overflow of a dam.

It is water/sunlight stored over a large area and a long period of time.

The flow is concentrated and dense.

So what the concentrated overflow of a dam allows you to do, rainfall cannot match by far.

Oil is like a dam that holds 150 million years of sunlight ready to burn at a go.

Just one day's worth of burning oil is equivalent to using 7 years worth of the total solar energy that reaches the Earth. That amounts to approximately 2500 times the rate at which it is reaching us. This point itself, if acknowledged, settles the issue of how little alternatives can do.

But for now, let us just register that this introduces us to another quality that different kinds of energies may have. They can be dilute or dense. This is called **Energy Density**.

That brings us to **ENERGY RULE #3 - ENERGY DENSITY:** **The Energy Density of the alternative must compare with the Energy Density of oil.**

Some people argue around this energy density problem as such: if these alternatives are collecting dilute energy, then we can make up by having more of them. Like more solar panels and more windmills. This is called "scaling up". According to these people, this should solve the problem.

Well, that is exactly what the governments and the alternative energy advocates and the energy venture capitalists have been trying so hard to do for the last 2 decades. Every effort has been made, including steep and generous government subsidies and tax breaks, to encourage the growth or "scaling up" of alternative energies. Yet this is how far we have reached in 2011.

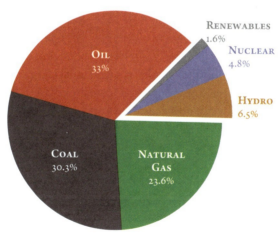

Global Energy Production

BP Statistical Review of World Energy 2012

A mere total of 13% is renewable energy and the balance 87 % is still fossil fuels (coal, gas & petroleum). Nuclear and Hydro together stand at 11.3%. And worse, the biggest hopes of solar and wind and other renewables add up to merely 1.6% of global energy production. There obviously seems to be some aspect of reality that is not allowing the use of alternative energies to go up. This limiting factor is measured as **Scalability**.

Scalability limits are different for each kind of alternative. But they are definitely there. For instance, solar panels need ground area, reliable sunlight, availability of silicon, etc. Windmills need suitable locations with winds above a critical minimum speed for a sufficient number of days. Many of the other touted options such as algae diesel have been tested for 50 years in labs, but the problem still remains of making it on a large scale to be viable and contributing.

So we arrive at **ENERGY RULE #4 - SCALABILITY: The alternative has to be scalable.**

Moving on, we find that there is an even larger issue that all alternatives lack. And this one nails them all decisively.

NONE of the alternatives give any of the byproducts that oil gives us such as bitumen, plastics, fertilizers, lubricants or pharmaceuticals on which the complete fabric of our Modern Industrial World is designed and built.

This huge implication is often slighted but is of astounding importance. It is equivalent to finding another alternative to water to run our human body which constitutes about 60% water. And if you cannot find water then it would require nothing less than a redesign and rebuilding of our body around a new liquid. This is clearly a difficult task. The same applies to the Modern Industrial World. We would have to do nothing less than redesign and rebuild it around the new alternatives. And where is the energy to achieve that going to come from?

So that needs to be embodied as another rule.

ENERGY RULE #5 - OIL BYPRODUCTS: The alternative energy option must give us the byproducts of oil crucial to building, running and maintaining our Modern Industrial World.

Let us put all the rules together so we get our minds around it.

ENERGY RULE #1 - NET ENERGY (ERoEI): The Net Energy gained has to be suitably high for an alternative to be viable.

ENERGY RULE #2 - OIL DEPENDENCY: The alternative must not be dependent on oil and its price.

ENERGY RULE #3 - ENERGY DENSITY : The energy density of the alternative must compare with the Energy Density of oil.

ENERGY RULE #4 - SCALABILITY: The alternative has to be scalable.

ENERGY RULE #5 - OIL BYPRODUCTS: The alternative energy option must give the byproducts of oil crucial to building, running and maintaining our Modern Industrial World.

Sadly we may see that all alternatives fail most of the rules above and that is what is curbing their wider usage. That is why I call alternative energies False Solutions.

But maybe they fail because of how we framed the Problem. Namely, we asked, "how can we run our current Modern Industrial World on alternatives exactly as it runs right now on oil?"

So naturally, we expect the Solution to be that alternatives, by part or complete replacement, will be able to run our world in the present manner of exponential growth post peak oil. This means that we expect to run our businesses, factories, industries, transportation, homes, agriculture, etc. pretty much along past exponential trends, even as oil production declines.

Above all, we expect that our economies and markets will continue growing, that we will get return on investment year after year and that the conventional laws of economic growth will be maintained.

We expect all this to happen with the ONLY exception that we will be powering our world by alternatives instead of oil.

To expect Alternative Energies to do this is impossible! And they end up being False Solutions. So you pose the problem wrongly and you get False Solutions.

By this I don't mean that there is no place for alternative energies in our future world. What I mean is that Alternative Energies have upper limits imposed by thermodynamic laws, cost, scale and applications. That is why they end up giving much less than the oil that went in to make them. So they fail most of the Energy Rules mentioned.

Pretty much like the new, lower salary job.

So what should you do when you simply have to go for a low salary job and there is no chance of ever getting back to a higher salary job?

You have to adjust your lifestyle. Scale down! This conclusion for alternative energies can be summed up as:

- *Alternative Energies cannot run the Modern Industrial World in the manner, cost and scale that we have designed and become used to.*

- *Sensibly used alternatives can fill important niches but it intrinsically requires scaling down our gross energy usage.*

- *This means Economic Shrinkage cannot be averted. Only managed in a non-disastrous way. Yes, growth died with the advent of Peak Oil and no combination of alternative energies can save that.*

What a pessimistic outlook, one might feel, but it is interesting to examine this a bit closer. Optimistic and Pessimistic were the only 2 viewpoints that our world recognized when we had plenty of oil and resources to fulfill our wildest concepts and dreams. Then we could make-do with only two outlooks. Either you were an optimist or if you said something that optimists did not like or did not agree with, then you were a pessimist.

There was no slot called a Realist.

Why not? Because we had nothing to do with reality. Because we were concept-based, remember? We just assumed that we needed to "conceive" and it would all be there. The Earth was obliged to surrender to our "human ingenuity" requirements. It was all about the Mind... and the Body had to comply.

So today we are pretty much trying to do the same with our approach to alternative energies. Just conceive an alternative energy solution and the laws of thermodynamics (physical reality) are obliged to comply.

Peak Oil and the subsequent energy decline have changed all this and suddenly there is a new respectability in being a realist. A realist is not a pessimist. He just has far more respect for reality and is willing to change his concepts and lifestyles to be in tune with it.

As Ayn Rand said, *"We can evade reality, but we cannot evade the consequences of evading reality"*.

The next section helps us evaluate in detail if we are indeed evading reality.

Types of Alternative Energy Options

The Alternative Energies being discussed these days fall into 3 categories.

Other Fossil Fuels are coal and natural gas. They do not form a direct replacement for oil but do already exist in nature. Please note that they are already bearing the burden of running a large part of the Modern Industrial World.

 **Liquid Fuel Alternatives** like Bio-fuels (Ethanol) or fuel extracted from tar-sands and oil-shale.

Though very poor performers, these are counted as most vital because they can directly replace oil and therefore stand a chance to contribute to running the Modern Industrial World the way it is built.

These fuel alternatives however don't exist in nature. They have to be produced.

 **Electricity Alternatives** like Solar, Wind, Hydro, Nuclear, Geothermal, Waves, Tides, Fusion and Fuel Cells.

They all only generate electricity and they need an oil and fossil-fuel based infrastructure that needs to be assembled, run and maintained.

1. Other Fossil Fuels: Coal and Natural Gas
Coal

Let us start with a rude reminder – coal and natural gas are both fossil fuels that are already bearing their own burden of running the industrial world and have their own impending peaks. They are therefore not alternatives in a strict sense.

In the case of coal, we have been hearing that there are 150 years of coal supplies at current rates of consumption. Please remind yourself two things that are needed to keep economic growth going as in the case of oil:

1. It is the peak production that matters, not how much of the resource is left.

2. We are consuming coal exponentially and a 150 year estimate will actually be gone in the space of about 43 years. Not 150 years! Folks, please don't forget the power of the exponential.

A large part of those 43 years will be spent doing the bell curve of coal just like oil.

So as coal is already a fossil fuel contributor in our modern industrial world, it is not an alternative in the strict sense but has already been a co-player in providing our energy needs all this while. And so now with oil having reached peak, coal will have to bear a greater burden.

This spells doom in the face of global warming and implies that we don't really mind if our planet gets fried, just as long as we can keep running the business of growth as usual. It is delusional to believe that coal has all of a sudden become a clean alternative when it is still giving off a huge quantity of CO_2 and other pollutants.

Earlier, coal used to be mined with what seemed a gentleman's code of conduct. You actually dug the good stuff out. But these days we do something that looks like the photo below.

Photo courtesy James Goodman, ilovemountains.org

It is called "mountain top removal"!

Now that is real progress! Just blast the whole mountain top off and keep our Modern Industrial World on the growth path.

Maybe someone should organize special holiday packages to witness the progress in "clean coal" technology.

How about the beautiful and pristine Appalachia mountains (photo above) for starters.

Oops… sorry, this is a slightly outdated photo of Appalachia.

Yes, this photo above, is where you will be spending your special-price, all-paid holiday. Appalachia – which has become a desert after intensive mountain top removal. Its rivers have poisoned to get to what we dare call "clean" coal.

A couple of parting points about coal.

- Radioactive material released by a large coal burning electric plant would be enough to build two atomic bombs.

- Mercury pollution is another one of the main consequences of burning coal and is blamed for 60,000 annual cases of brain damage in newborn children in the U.S.

CONCLUSION: Resorting to coal to chase the perpetual growth promise is like taking a giant step backwards in time however using a neon-sign that says "Running on Clean Coal"!

Other Fossil Fuel Alternatives

Natural Gas

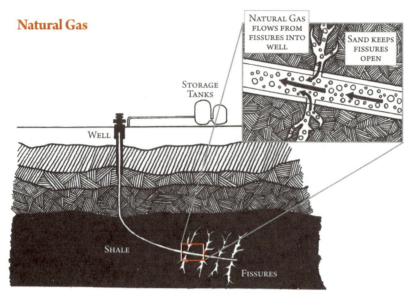

The latest euphoria in the U.S. is a new technology called hydraulic fracturing, or fracking, that releases natural gas trapped in shale rock that was earlier inaccessible. This is done by creating fractures in the rock with a mixture of water, sand and toxic chemicals pumped under high pressure.

Undoubtedly fracking technology has extended the game but not averted the inevitability of peak oil or its impacts on economic growth. This is evident by the fact that though there is a surge in natural gas production in the U.S., it has not dented oil prices one bit. Crude oil prices are steady over $100 per barrel even in the midst of an enduring economic recession. This is simply because natural gas is not much of a replacement for liquid fuels which are the linchpin energy source for the Modern Industrial World. Surplus cheap natural gas therefore cannot keep the growth engine running.

For the reader interested in a detailed evaluation of the dangers of investing too much hope in natural gas, I highly recommend a book by Richard Heinberg titled *Snake Oil: How Fracking's False Promise of Plenty Imperils Our Future.*

Meanwhile let us look at how natural gas performs in the context of our Energy Rules:

- To start with, it fails **ENERGY RULE #3 - Energy Density** as a huge volume of 157 cubic metres of natural gas has the same energy equivalent as only one barrel of oil.

144

- Natural gas also fails **ENERGY RULE #5 - Byproducts**. It does not give us any oil byproducts so greatly needed to build and maintain our Modern Industrial World.

- And finally, it fails **ENERGY RULE #4 - Scalability.** Natural gas wells are declining at much steeper rates than oil wells. A study by The Association for the Study of Peak Oil (ASPO) revealed that unless more wells were drilled, production would fall by 38% within a year. In that scenario, 1,600 new wells would be required per year to maintain production at its current level.

And now the environmental impacts of fracking:

- Fracking methods require millions of litres of water, pumped from natural water bodies and transported in large trucks running on diesel. The fracking fluid resulting from each individual process is laden with thousands of kilograms of chemicals at levels that are frequently unacceptably higher than the level that U.S. federal safety standards stipulate.

- Endocrine Disruption Exchange tests have concluded that 93% of these chemicals are reported to affect health if ingested, inhaled or if they enter in contact with the skin. Among these chemicals are methanol, benzene, naphthalene, ethylbenzene, polycyclic aromatic hydrocarbons, ethylene glycol, formaldehyde, glycol ethers, hydrochloric acid, toluene, xylene, sodium hydroxide and others. They are considered caustic, carcinogenic, mutagenic and teratogenic and 43% are endocrine disruptors which mimic hormones or block hormones in the human body causing infertility, ADHD, autism, diabetes and thyroid disorders. Even childhood and adult cancers have been found to be linked to endocrine disruptors through fetal exposure. [4]

CONCLUSION: Natural gas by fracking with its low energy density, high well depletion rates and inability to substitute liquid fuels is evidently unable to prevent the decline of economic growth. Yet the aggressive and dangerous measure of fracking being practiced relentlessly is a sure way to kill whole communities by ground water and air contamination with dangerous chemicals.

Other Fossil Fuel Alternatives

2. Liquid Fuel Alternatives: Bio Fuel (Ethanol), Tar Sands, Shale Oil.

Alternatives like ethanol, tar-sands and shale oil are the current darlings of the alternative energy struggle because they actually give liquid fuel and can form a direct replacement for petroleum that is crucial to transport, as well as to other aspects of running our world the way it is designed.

These sources are plants and food grains, tar-sands and shale deposits. This is the reason why they are called unconventional sources of liquid fuel as they have to be extracted from deposits or organic matter.

Therefore, they are extremely labor, resource and energy intensive to produce and refine. This translates into higher production costs and up to three times more greenhouse gas emissions per barrel. [5]

All these alternatives fail **ENERGY RULE #1 - Net Energy (ERoEI)** meaning that the Net Energy or the Energy Returned on Energy Invested (ERoEI)can at best be marginal – you put a lot of oil energy to produce them and get marginal energy return when they are used. Many studies show that in many cases, we actually get less energy burning them than the sum of the energy invested in producing them. So actually they are net losers of energy. The only reason why we are so desperately pushing for them is because they come closest in replacing petroleum as a liquid fuel and our world is largely designed to run on liquid fuel.

They all fail **ENERGY RULE #2 - Oil Dependency**. They all require oil and other fossil fuels to extract and refine. Besides, the environmental implications in each case are monumental. Considering any of these alternatives is a sure sign of desperation to keep the world running as it does presently, at any cost to life on this planet. The whole enterprise borders on insanity.

Bio Fuel (Ethanol)

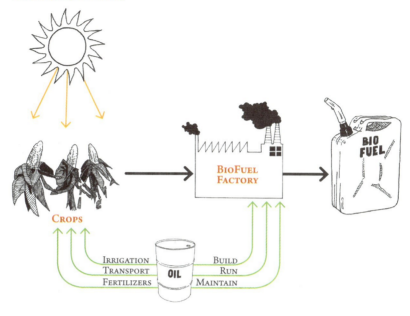

Ethanol is obtained by growing food grains and oilseed crops that are used to create liquid fuel and is currently being aggressively advertised as one of the most promising liquid fuel solutions. The common man has accepted that ethanol will soon be a true replacement for oil. This is a fantasy that is not based on scientific facts and can therefore be dangerous to believe. Bio fuel fails to follow the following energy rules:

- Bio fuel fails **ENERGY RULE #2 - Oil Dependency.** It requires oil and other fossil fuels to grow the crops and further to extract and refine bio fuel. Huge quantities of nitrogen-based fertilizer are used for corn crops used to obtain ethanol. Additionally, ethanol is highly corrosive and can therefore not be transported in pipelines, necessitating delivery by tanker trucks that run on diesel fuel. [6]

- Bio fuel fails **ENERGY RULE #4 - Scalability.** Since ethanol is produced through grain and oilseed farming, harvests are being used to fuel our cars instead of feeding ourselves. As David Strahan, author of *The Last Oil Shock* puts it, *"Even if we devoted all our cropland to biofuel production, we would only produce a quarter of our current fuel consumption. We could all starve to death in a traffic jam"*. Primarily because of this trend, the price of food around the world has doubled since 2007 (post Peak Oil).

Liquid Fuel Alternatives

- Last but not least, bio fuels also fail the very first **ENERGY RULE #1 - Net Energy (ERoEI)**, which is the most important one. Indeed, the final knockdown to bio fuels is that it takes 4.9 litres of petroleum to obtain a meagre 3.8 litres of ethanol!!

As if failing these energy rules were not enough, bio fuel also generates a certain amount of environmental concerns. Consider this:

- Nitrogen-based fertilizers, used to aggressively boost bio fuel crops, cause soil and water damage as well as public health concerns. Fertilizer runoff has been killing life in the Gulf of Mexico for decades, while contaminated ground water used for public water supply in the U.S. has been known to increase the thyroid cancer risk in women.

- Dedicating forest land to growing bio fuel crops causes deforestation while soy biodiesel and corn ethanol actually double their carbon emissions compared to petrol. This of course contributes to global warming. And so it is devastating the planet instead of preserving it, as most ethanol proponents claim.

CONCLUSION: Ethanol is a net negative-energy solution that comes with a huge environmental cost. This crazy solution is being promoted so aggressively simply because it gives us liquid fuel that the world so desperately needs. Now let us also take a look at its sister liquid fuel contenders - tar sand and shale oil.

Tar Sands

Photos courtesy Colin Baines, The Co-operative Group

Before   *After*

If bio fuel was a suicidal solution, tar sands can be compared to committing cold-blooded carnage.

First of all tar sands are not oil that can be readily used. They are in fact a mixture of clay, sand, water and bitumen: an extremely viscous type of oil. Contrary to pumping oil out from the Earth, the oil in tar sands requires energy-intensive refining before it can be used as fuel. This energy we get from copious quantities of natural gas (also a fossil fuel) to generate steam that separates the oil from the sand.

Pushing tar sands as an intelligent and reasonable alternative is an insane, desperate and atrocious stance, as is best illustrated by Dr. Robert Skinner, (Oxford Institute of Energy, speaking in 2003). He says:

> *I hope that I don't have the following conversation with my granddaughter twenty years from now:*
>
> *"Grandpa, did you really do that"?*
>
> *"Do 'what', Masha"?*
>
> *"Did you take natural gas from the Arctic, down to Alberta, to boil water, to make steam, to melt tar out of the oil sands, then use more natural gas to make hydrogen, to make the tar molecules into petrol, so that North Americans could drive four ton vehicles five kilometers to sports clubs to spend fifteen minutes riding stationary bikes? Did you really do that, Grandpa"?*
>
> *"Ahhhh…, yes, Masha, I am afraid we did".*

Liquid Fuel Alternatives

This prospect summarizes the insanity of tar sands. Tar sands fail the following energy rules:

- From the above it is obvious that producing oil from tar sands violates **ENERGY RULE #1 - Net Energy (EROEI)**. The Energy Returned on Energy Invested is at best marginal.

- It also violates **ENERGY RULE #2 - Oil Dependency**, as every step of extraction and production is immensely fossil fuel dependent.

And now consider the appalling environmental impact of tar sands on the Earth.

- Extracting tar sands requires the felling of large areas of ancient boreal forests. Greenpeace estimates that annual carbon dioxide emissions caused by tar sands go beyond 80 million tons of CO_2, which is more than that currently produced by all of Canada's vehicles. This is hardly a recipe for dealing with global warming. [7]

- Huge quantities of water with even larger quantities of precious natural gas are burnt to generate poor quality crude oil. The amount of natural gas used for example is enough to heat more than 3 million Canadian homes. And it takes between two to four barrels of water to produce one barrel of tar sand oil. [8]

- Tar sands' thirst for water has produced large amounts of toxic wastewater. The second-largest dam in the world was built to hold toxic waste back from flowing from the tar sands to the Athabasca River. [9]

- As a result, Alberta's per capita greenhouse gas emissions are higher than any other country in the world.

It would probably be simpler to just drop a neutron bomb on the area.

Matt Simmons, author of the book *Twilight in the Desert*, describes this futile enterprise quite suitably. He says: *"Gentlemen, we have just turned gold into lead"*.

Dr. Frederic Malter, from the Munich Center for the Economics of Ageing, put that a bit more honestly and plainly:

> "...society's excitement about tar sand is like an alcoholic coming into a bar and finding the taps have run dry. But after years of customers spilling beer on the carpet, he kneels down and tries to wring out a few drops of booze from the carpet".

CONCLUSION: Tar sands is nothing short of a criminal attempt to brush aside over 50 years of environmental awareness to promote a negative Net Energy solution. Once again it reveals the desperation of the situation, thus confirming the peak oil argument: we are at the top of the oil curve, and the era of cheap oil is now gone and done with.

Oil Shale

Photo from U.S. National Archives

Let us get one thing clear – oil shale in fact does not contain oil as such, but a solid organic material called kerogen. Therefore oil shale needs to be converted to shale oil through a very energy intensive process.

- Oil shale fails the very first test. It violates **ENERGY RULE #1 - Net Energy (EROEI)**. Producing material that resembles liquid oil requires burning natural gas and heating kerogen to above 300 degrees centigrade, which itself requires a high energy consumption process. The National Resources Defense Council citing Rand Corporation estimates that generating 100,000 barrels of oil from

151

oil shale would require energy the equivalent of a new power plant capable of serving a city of 500,000 people!

- Oil shale fails **ENERGY RULE #2 - Oil Dependency**. It requires extensive oil infrastructure to extract and produce.

Now let us consider the environmental effects of oil shale:

- The method requires flattening vast areas of land, thereby seriously damaging wildlife and vegetation in the area.

- Each barrel of oil obtained from oil shale requires 2.1 to 5.2 barrels of water taken from already water-challenged regions. The same amount then becomes contaminated wastewater due to the extraction process and must be disposed of responsibly.

- And besides this damage, Worldwatch Institute reports that oil shale extraction releases lead, nitrogen oxides and sulfur dioxide for which proper disposal is an issue and can be ecologically catastrophic.

CONCLUSION: The perpetual promise of oil shale is best expressed by Brian J. Fleay, from the Institute of Sustainability and Technology Policy at Murdoch University (Australia), who states: *"Shale oil is like a mirage that retreats as it is approached"*. No wonder production of oil from oil shale has been attempted at various times for nearly 100 years but is yet unviable. Shale oil is, as the saying goes: "The fuel of the future and always will be".

3. Electricity Alternatives:
Solar, Wind, Hydro, Nuclear, Hydrogen, Fuel Cells, Geothermal, Wave, Tidal, and Fusion

So we have worked our way down to the third option of alternatives – **Electricity Alternatives.** These are most often mentioned as the first choice of getting off oil dependency but there are traps that avid solar, wind and nuclear proponents overlook. The 2 curses haunting most electricity alternatives are **Intermittency** and **Storage**, and so cannot provide a steady base-load that is crucial to serving our modern electricity demands.

Hydro, Nuclear and Geothermal are not affected by this as they can supply a steady base-load. But they have other limitations we will examine later.

Sun-based alternatives, like solar and wind, are intermittent because of day and night, cloudy and clear skies and are dependent on season and latitude. Even in a normal day of sunlight the effective hours of sunlight with appropriate declination angle are limited to about 6 hours – 10 to 4 pm.

Availability of the sun also affects the wind and waves at night. So all solar, wind, wave and tidal – are intrinsically intermittent and therefore vulnerable to storage.

Electrical energy can only be stored in batteries and they are expensive, inefficient and heavy. The energy that batteries can store is also very limited. Check how batteries compare with other energy sources in the graph on the next page.

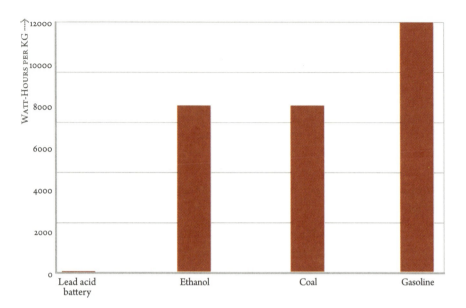

We would require one ton of lead-acid storage batteries to compete with the energy provided by approximately 4 litres of petrol!

To put that in daily perspective it would take 15 tons of batteries to provide the same amount of energy obtained from 60 litres of petrol in a car's tank.

You can clearly see that any electricity alternative relying on battery storage is facing a failure of **ENERGY RULE #3 - Energy Density**.

Based on the observations above and on the fact that batteries would add a significant amount of weight to any vehicle running on them, we see that there is no battery system that can efficiently move heavy farm machinery to support modern agriculture or trucks, ships and planes that form the back-bone of transportation in the modern industrial world.

Batteries also become virtually useless in extremely low temperatures and need to be replaced every few years at a large cost.

These are significant constraints to begin with and it is best to know they exist before we start diving into the aspects of each electricity alternative.

Solar

Solar energy of course comes from the Sun, which to us seems like an unlimited and ever-bountiful source. The viability of solar however is not how much sunlight reaches the Earth but mainly the rate at which you can harvest and store it, and at what cost.

- Solar energy is a **low density energy**, with low conversion efficiency (about 15%). This makes it fail **ENERGY RULE #3 - Energy Density.** Solar needs extensive areas for the installation of solar panels. Therefore, around towns, cities and industrial areas, where it is most needed, the price of land makes this an exorbitant option.

- No wonder that despite extremely generous subsidies by governments, solar and wind combined are only 1.3% of the global energy production. So clearly, it fails **ENERGY RULE #4 - Scalability**.

- Solar energy fails **ENERGY RULE #2 - Oil Dependency** as eventually solar panels and storage batteries themselves are made using an oil energy-based infrastructure. Therefore solar will always be oil dependent. As the price of oil goes up, so does that of solar panels and batteries.

- Solar fails **ENERGY RULE #5 - Oil Byproducts**. Solar panels only generate electricity and do not provide any of the oil-based byproducts.

- Solar energy is unable to provide a steady load of electricity that would be needed for heavy current usage such as fridges, motors, electrical industrial machinery or air-conditioning units, let alone running any part of our transportation such as ships, planes, trucks and trains, whether it be on direct solar energy or batteries.

CONCLUSION: Solar energy is intermittent, low density, expensive, oil dependent, has limits of scalability and generates only electricity. It can certainly be useful at small scale and personal levels but can never keep the Modern Industrial World running the way it does on oil or perpetuate the growth paradigm. Therefore solar is not an alternative in the sense that most solar advocates are imagining.

Electricity Alternatives

155

Wind

Wind is a secondary effect of the sun. The sun heats the air that turns to wind which then turns turbines that generate electricity. So this energy source is similar to solar in that it is not dependable given that sunlight is intermittent.

- The Net Energy or ERoEI can be reasonably high (around 15 to 20 times) depending on the site. But producing only electricity, which is no significant replacement for oil and its by-products. So wind fails **ENERGY RULE #5 - Oil Byproducts.**

- Wind fails **ENERGY RULE #4 - Scalability** as there are very limited suitable inland sites for installing windmills. Therefore at best, wind is only a modest help in the total world energy supply.

- And finally, the complete wind farm enterprise is built, run and maintained using an oil infrastructure and byproducts. So wind energy fails **ENERGY RULE #2 - Oil Dependency.**

- Similarly to solar energy, large amounts of wind-generated electricity cannot be stored and remain unreliable. Wind can therefore not provide a base-load necessary to electricity consumption in our Modern Industrial World.

And now the environmental costs.

- Apart from this, wind-generated power causes several environmental concerns. The most important windmill sites tend to be located in areas where air funnels through the hills, which are also commonly flyways for birds. After all, birds intuitively follow the flight of least effort using wind currents to their advantage and this leads them into the windmills. Not by chance but by design.

CONCLUSION: Wind energy is intermittent, low density, expensive, oil dependent, has limits of scalability and generates only electricity. It is sorely dependent on Government subsidies for viability. It can never keep the Modern Industrial World running the way it is on oil or perpetuate the paradigm of growth. Therefore, it is not an alternative in the sense that most wind advocates are imagining.

Hydro

Hydro electricity, generated by dams, has been originally considered as a green, clean and environmentally friendly source of energy. It has been here for the longest time but the world has discovered the down side of large dams. So here goes.

- First of all, large dams are built on a mammoth infrastructure that runs on oil. Right from the construction, machinery, installation and power-generation to its distribution and maintenance. So dams fail **ENERGY RULE #2 - Oil Dependency**.

- Dams fail **ENERGY RULE #4 - Scalability**. Most of the suitable dam sites are already constructed so (thankfully) dams cannot be scaled up significantly – a blessing in disguise.

- The end product is electricity, not a replacement for oil, and of course we get none of oil's vital byproducts. It is therefore a mere illusion that hydro-electricity is any replacement for oil. It fails **ENERGY RULE #5 - Oil Byproducts.**

And now the enivironmental costs:

- Environmental destruction is silent and incalculable. Rivers are the arteries of the Earth and large dams kill a river downstream. So by concept a large dam is equivalent to blocking an artery in the body of the Earth. Visualize gangrene in a limb where the blood supply is cut off. Would you do it to your body? Certainly not! Then why do we allow large dams to kill the body of the Earth?

- All dams finally silt and so have a finite life. But the river is dead forever. Sedimentation is inevitable and in fact, reports are revealing that reservoirs are silting up at rates much faster than calculated. Silt deposits have reduced water storage capacity by 30 to 40 %. In a few hundred years most large dams will be concrete walls holding mud on one side. [10]

- Useful wetlands, which are usually valuable for farming, have become flooded and are not available for food production.

- Upstream, human settlements and wildlife are displaced and destroyed by reservoir flooding. The resulting urban migration creates slums and flagrant social disparity in large cities.

Electricity Alternatives

- Approximately 50 million people (40 million in the case of large dams) were displaced by big projects in 50 years of independence, according to N. C. Saxena, then Secretary of the Planning Commission, quoted in Dams, Displacement, Policy and Law in India, 1999.

Here's how Arundhati Roy, Booker Prize winning author, puts these numbers in sharp perspective in her essay titled *The Greater Common Good* on large dams:

> *"Fifty million is more than the population of Gujarat. Almost three times the population of Australia. More than three times the number of refugees that Partition created in India. Ten times the number of Palestinian refugees. The Western world today is convulsed over the future of one million people who have fled from Kosovo".*

And as if that was not enough:

- Even all downstream communities are devastated without even being considered as project-affected, so they have no chance of receiving compensation. They don't even feature in the numbers above.

- Water is privatized and diverted to rich farmers, industries and metros that have the most wasteful practices for water in known history. Rich farmers grow water-thirsty crops like sugarcane – not a food crop but instead a crop for a completely ancillary and redundant sugar industry. Care to browse through some figures on diabetes in the Modern Industrial World?

So we shut our eyes to the havoc of large dams which proudly compete with the holocaust. Because we all have been sold the great illusion of development. And of course it is not our home and villages that are being flooded. It is only of those 40 million souls, and counting, who were meant to be sacrificed in the great project of nation-building, while being Earth destroying.

CONCLUSION: Large dams are weapons of mass destruction benignly labelled "temples of modern India". They generate only electricity at a huge economic, environmental and social cost while permanently killing complete rivers. Dam building is the most monumental and structured enterprise of killing our planet. Many first world countries are actively working on dismantling them. But that costs money and energy too!

Nuclear Plants

Nuclear holds a special science fiction aura of sanctity around it despite recent cracks in its image. Nuclear plants generate electricity by generating heat through a radioactive reaction. The water, turned to steam, passes through a turbine to generate electricity. The commonly held belief that nuclear is clean and cheap has been shattered by decades of actual experience. Nuclear energy is in deep trouble in all respects today.

- The **Net Energy** or **ERoEI** has never been estimated honestly. This is because of the complexity of the process. Total energy needed for decommissioning is now estimated to be approximately 50 percent more than the energy needed in the original construction. [11]

- The oil dependency story is the same with nuclear energy as with all other alternatives – it is totally dependent on an oil infrastructure. So it fails ENERGY RULE #2 - **Oil Dependency.**

- Once again nuclear does not give us any by-products of oil on which our Modern Industrial World is built, run and maintained. So it fails ENERGY RULE #5 - **Oil Byproducts.**

And now the environmental costs:

- The used up radioactive rods must cool off in ponds that need a reliable electricity supply to keep them stirred and topped up with water in order to stop radioactive fuel from drying out and catching fire. This would be increasingly difficult and costly to sustain in an energy depleting world.

- Later, all this radioactive waste material needs to be packed by robots into high security canisters lined with steel, lead, and pure electrolytic copper which will then be buried in immense and seemingly stable geological depositories.

- The energy needed to manufacture these canisters is estimated to be approximately equal to the energy needed to build the reactor in the first place. [12] Has anyone bothered to tally that to energy invested?

- Apart from energy considerations, nuclear energy is extremely capital intensive. Nuclear only became viable because of heavy subsidies from the government. Uranium is required, which is a

Electricity Alternatives

159

rare and finite source with its own production peak. Since 2006, uranium prices have already more than doubled.

- Nuclear is often touted as a carbon-free method of generating electricity. That is the same sleight of hand that makes a number of alternative energies look benign, given that only the final stage is being factored. But what about all that goes on before and after?

- Elaborate and expensive radio-active waste disposal techniques are only a way of deferring present responsibilities onto future generations who will eventually discover and be exposed to its radiation.

- The entire process of mining, processing, enriching, treating and disposing of uranium has significant greenhouse impacts. One example is how uranium enrichment requires large volumes of uranium hexafluoride and other halogenated compounds. These are greenhouse gases that have the 10,000 times the potential of carbon dioxide in regard to global warming.

No wonder nuclear power development has been stopped in the United States. Elsewhere, some countries are abandoning nuclear power (e.g. Sweden, Germany, Japan), whereas others who are pursuing it (e.g. Russia) are having second thoughts.

For a thorough demolition of nuclear power in the context of peak oil and climate change, refer to Fleming, D. (2007), *The Lean Guide to Nuclear Energy: a Life Cycle in Trouble*.

CONCLUSION: The nuclear energy façade is wearing thin with the spate of recent disasters. An honest evaluation of benefits and viabilities therefore will dawn on us tragically only in retrospect – as the energy needed to maintain it declines. To camouflage nuclear as a "clean" or "safe" alternative is a clear sign of desperation in the face of Peak Oil.

Hydrogen

The widespread belief that hydrogen is going to save the day is a good example of how grossly misled people are. Free hydrogen does not exist on this planet. It takes energy from some other source to generate it. Therefore it is a carrier of energy and not a source of energy.

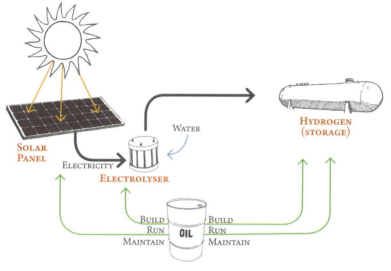

- The current source of hydrogen is natural gas (CH_4), which is a hydrocarbon. It requires more energy to break a hydrogen bond than what can be obtained from the hydrogen produced and therefore hydrogen fails **ENERGY RULE #1 - Net Energy (ERoEI).**

- So putting the infrastructure in place to efficiently and cheaply produce and store hydrogen on the same widespread basis as oil and its derivatives today, is an enormous, costly, and long term task.

- Apart from this, hydrogen is highly explosive and therefore difficult to handle, having to be compressed and cooled at extremely cold temperatures in order to be transported and stored. It is therefore obviously not a convenient replacement for gasoline!

CONCLUSION: Hydrogen is a pseudo-alternative solution and can never replace or significantly contribute in an oil-based economy.

Fuel Cells

Fuel cells are not a source of energy. They are like a generator that needs hydrogen to run, to be able to produce electricity and you have already seen what a grand illusion hydrogen itself is as an alternative.

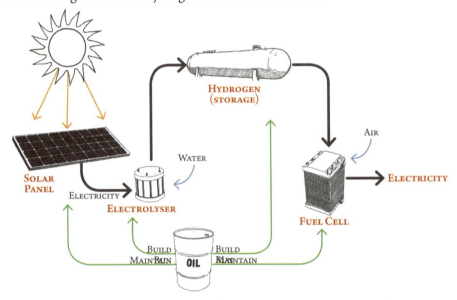

In a fuel cell, hydrogen and oxygen are fed to the anode and cathode, respectively, of each cell. Electrons stripped from hydrogen produce electricity.

- The basic problem of hydrogen fuel cells is that we expend more energy in generating the hydrogen than the energy generated in a fuel cell with the same hydrogen as fuel. So fuel cells intrinsically fail **ENERGY RULE #1 - Net Energy (ERoEI)**.

- If we use fossil fuels to generate hydrogen, using the methane-steam or electrolysis of water methods, we will see no benefit over directly using fossil fuel. So fuel cells also fail **ENERGY RULE #2 - Oil Dependency**.

- And after all that, fuel cells only give electricity, and none of the byproducts of petroleum that shape our world. Yes, fuel cells most definitely fail **ENERGY RULE #5 - Oil Byproducts**.

CONCLUSION: I leave it to you to read up further on fuel cells and then figure out why there is such a great deal being made about them as an alternative source of energy.

Geothermal

Heat provided by the Earth is the source of Geothermal energy. First, water is pumped down to the Earth's heat reservoir and is later pumped up to generate electricity.

- Few places in the world can find steam or water at very high temperatures close to the surface of the Earth to exploit economically. So how much can you possibly scale up this solution? It basically fails ENERGY RULE #4 - **Scalability** from the start.

- The end product is electricity – not any substitute for the byproducts of oil, thus failing ENERGY RULE #5 - **Byproducts**.

- It is obvious that the complete Geothermal enterprise runs on oil, so it fails ENERGY RULE#2 - **Oil Dependency**.

- Geothermal power generating site reservoirs around the world are now in decline, as geothermal energy-based electric power wears out reservoirs faster than their ability to recharge.

CONCLUSION: Geothermal will always be a marginal player in the alternative energy solution balance sheet and therefore it cannot halt the inversion of the economic paradigm from growth to shrinkage.

Wave energy

Wave energy installations have been attempted in very few cases. Waves are not a dependable source. The environment in which these systems have to work is very risky and unpredictable. Also, sea water is highly corrosive and long term maintenance promises to be a real challenge.

Apart from this, the end product is only electricity, and producing it in significant quantities from waves seems a very remote, expensive and difficult prospect.

Though there are several experimental projects around the world testing different types of systems the results have been extremely modest.

Conclusion: The possibility of wave-generated energy being a worthy solution is rather bleak. We may wonder how much longer mankind will squander large sums on futile experiments before we finally accept the limits imposed by the laws of energy.

Electricity Alternatives

Tidal Power

Tidal power, also called tidal energy, is a form of hydropower that converts the energy of tides into electricity. A site that is capable of producing a valuable quantity of tidal power requires very specific conditions such as a suitably high tide, a particular coastline configuration and a narrow estuary which can be dammed. Such locations are very limited. And besides, the last 100 years have taught us what dams do to a river! So for a start, this is an irresponsible and desperate pursuit.

- Tidal power is not a significant power source. There is no data regarding **Net Energy** gained figures.

- Only about nine viable sites have been identified in the world. Two are now in use (Russia and France) and generate some electricity. So this solution fails **ENERGY RULE #4 - Scalability**.

- Tidal power generates only electricity and needs a huge oil infrastructure to maintain. So it also fails **ENERGY RULE #5 - Oil Byproducts**.

- Tidal power is intermittent so it would therefore only allow power generation for around 10 hours each day, when the tide is actually moving in or out.

- Salt water corrodes metal parts and makes it difficult to maintain tidal stream generators. Barrages across estuaries are extremely costly and difficult to maintain.

Tidal power production is not without affecting the environment:

- Damage to the environment is immeasurable and affects a very large area - many kilometers upstream and downstream.

- By blocking the normal flow of tides and by using turbines with rotating blades or leaking mechanical fluids, such as lubricants, tidal power production can harm or kill marine life.

CONCLUSION: Tidal power is a desperate high-tech and cost-intensive measure that is an unviable effort with enormous downsides that will be revealed with time.

Fusion

Fusion is the energy which powers the Sun. The problem is that it is known to happen at the temperature of the Sun, which ranges from about 10,000°C on its surface to an estimated 15 to 18 million degrees in the interior. In short, for fusion to work, we would need to replicate the temperature of the sun. No wonder fusion is an evasive solution that remains hypothetical or almost in the realm of science fiction.

For people resting their hopes on fusion at the crest of Peak Oil, I think it is time to get real! The patient is in the ICU and we are claiming that we are sure of finding a cure any minute because research has been going on for the last 50 years!

False Solution # 6: Human Ingenuity.
FALSE BELIEF: Human Intelligence is boundless.

When all of the above fail to I find people resorting to the last bastion of hope and belief - the infiniteness and infallibility of Human Ingenuity. Our cultural conditioning of open-ended optimism fails to admit that it was the same kind of human ingenuity that caused this mess. Our kind of human ingenuity and approach is quantity based and has clearly failed. We now need to redefine human ingenuity that goes beyond mere quantity and recognises and respects limits that this book has been underlining from the start.

So it is not about simply finding some ingenious means to run the same paradigm of limitless Perpetual Exponential Quantitative Growth but about accepting the eternal virtue of finiteness and interconnectedness that ecology, communities and living systems operate within.

So human ingenuity is a factor to consider but it takes a particular kind of human ingenuity to recognize this. And that kind of human ingenuity comes up with a different approach altogether.

This approach to human ingenuity is what this book advocates and we explore in a bit of detail in Chapter 5 - Transition.

Electricity Alternatives

Summing up the Fallacy of Alternatives

This was a quick review of the failure of our Alternative Energy hopes. A detailed examination is even more humbling but remains beyond the scope of this book.

The prime objective was to show why running our Modern Industrial World and our current financial paradigm of perpetual exponential growth is not possible with any combination of Alternative Energies. Only fossil fuels had the ability to allow us to operate highly complex systems at gigantic scales to permit exponential growth.

The public, business leaders and politicians (well versed in economics but NOT in energy principles) are all under the false assumption that oil depletion is a straightforward engineering problem of exactly the kind that technology and human ingenuity have so successfully solved before.

Sadly, even the scientific and technical community are misleading the general public by saying that it is just a matter of time, that science and technological innovations will actually beat the upper limits of geology and thermodynamics to solve the energy crisis.

This is impossible and that is what this whole chapter was all about.

In the next chapter we will move on to addressing the real predicament with real responses.

Part IV

The Third Curve
The Eternal Rhythm of the Universe

Vision of the Third Curve

So where do we go from here? How do we reconcile the unsolvable mess we appear to be in?

Maybe the answer lies in the notion of Limits.

I selected 2 curves to illustrate the dangers of not respecting limits.

The Exponential **Concept** of limitless money growth was an aberration and the CAUSE.

The Bell Curve **Reality** of excessive resource depletion was the symptom and the EFFECT.

And as we have seen, the Cause is unsustainable and the Effect undesirable.

The resulting disease is being felt in all life-signs soaring exponentially out of safe bounds.

Maybe we need to move beyond these 2 Curves to one that is embedded in nature – a behavioral curve of the universe.

This curve is sustainable and desirable because it intrinsically respects limits reflecting an energy and resource pattern that was naturally available to us before we started the one-way looting and burning of stored energy.

This I call the Third Curve.

We spoke of **Mind** and **Body**. Minds are unlimited but every body has limits that are defined by its own Third Curve – the limits between which its energy oscillates. These are the limits between which that body can function healthily as an organism. The body of an ant, a lion or even our Runner, each have their own Third Curve. Pumping them with extra energy beyond that limit is not going to help them. It will only end up breaking the delicate balance of energies on which they were meant to function.

169

We come back to our cultural blind spot of ignoring that the Earth is an organism. And therefore, the Earth has its own Third Curve. So it is not a question of how much energy we CAN find and burn in an illusion of success and progress, but it is a question of how much we SHOULD.

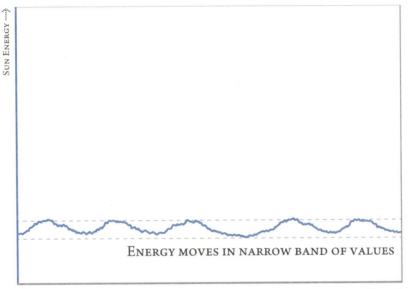

ENERGY MOVES IN NARROW BAND OF VALUES

The Third Curve of the living Earth faithfully follows the rhythm of our primary energy provider, the sun. Reliably it rises, peaks and ebbs only to rise again – the flush of nature governed by the sun.

This was how the Earth behaved for ages before we appeared and continues to do so. That was our budget for existence universally ordained.

As for growth – it was always meant to oscillate in gentle waves of highs and lows following the sun's energy. The smaller oscillations of day and night were superimposed on larger oscillations of seasons and the even larger oscillations of solar cycles.

Ever changing, yet ever remaining, in a narrow band of values. Nothing going to the sky and nothing going to zero. Those were the limits set by the universe for our actions, for our own benefit and for our survival.

Those were the limits respected by all other forms of life on this planet including our indigenous ancestors and the surviving indigenous cultures today that we are actively wiping out with our myth of progress and inverted view of well-being.

Violating all limits, modern civilization burnt every known form of stored sunlight, distorting the Third Curve exponentially to the extent that today we find ourselves in the unenviable position of Peak of Oil usage, Peak of Planetary Plundering and Peak of Delusion.

But return to the Third Curve is inevitable. Because that is the steady-state – the eternal rhythm of the universe.

It is not so surprising that by submitting and reverting to this eternal rhythm we also address in parallel the other pressing problems of ecological collapse and global warming.

The Third Curve is the pulse of all things in sync with the universe. By surrendering to it, we are allowing ourselves to be embraced by the very energies that put us here in the first place.

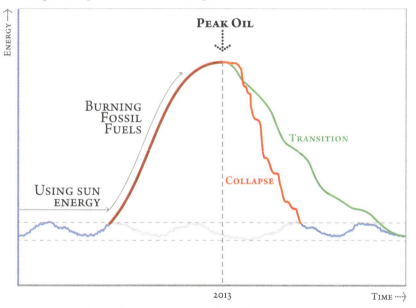

We have 2 paths to the Third Curve – **denial** or **acceptance** of peak oil.

The path through **denial** can certainly extend our moment at the top of the peak only to exacerbate our predicament leading to an eventual steep, and short chaotic **collapse**. Each attempt at flattening the curve to maintain status quo will result in a sudden sharp drop of collapse giving the descent a staircase shape. In the dying throes of denial, we would try every trick to kick-start flagging growth and in the process burn most of what could have actually saved some aspects of our present condition. The Earth, in this

171

state of the Third Curve, promises to be uninhabitable, as we would have lost most of our resources in fighting the descent rather than accepting it as an inevitability.

The path through acceptance can immediately start a smoother, longer and managed energy descent, which involves re-alignment of our economic paradigm, cultural beliefs, making sacrifices and bearing some degree of pain. This path will be gentler, less steep and give us time to adapt. It also entails a simultaneous understanding and movement towards the new world that is inevitable with a lower energy budget. We stand a much better chance of bypassing collapse and consciously shaping an unfamiliar but desirable future. This is the Transition that we will examine in the next chapter.

Part V

Transition
Rebuilding a Post Peak Oil World

Personal Dilemma about
Peak Oil & End of Growth

"Any intelligent fool can make things bigger, more complex, and more violent. It takes a touch of genius – and a lot of courage – to move in the opposite direction".

Albert Einstein

For us as architects of modern industrial civilization, the collective belief so far has been "big is beautiful, more is good, individualism is prime, one size fits all and accumulation first then charity". All this led to a particular kind of social structure, economics, laws, business model and therefore lifestyle.

We have to now first personally believe that small is beautiful, less is good, local is important, community is strength, sharing itself is charity and diversity is paramount.

This amounts to a huge shift in our cultural perspective. Not easy but then we are not talking about ease, are we? We are talking about what is likely to work in an energy declining world.

If the future appears gloomy, it is because we believe that the current way the world works is the only and best option. Sadly, we have been conditioned in such a way that we cannot see beyond the current paradigm of industrial growth. Any talk about the end of growth instantly evokes strong feelings of fear and hopelessness.

So then, what are we supposed to do?

At the end of one my lectures on this subject, a young lady, who acknowledged the argument of Peak Oil and the End of Growth, looked perturbed and said, "But what can I do as an individual? Should it not be up to the authorities or governments to take action?"

I told her that the effort of my lectures was an attempt towards individual realization first. Because growth has been the accepted economic paradigm so far, naturally the government in a democracy acts on what they believe we expect from them. If we ourselves believe in the old paradigm of perpetual growth, then surely that is what they will hand to us when we vote for them.

Therefore, before we expect any national and international response, we should make sure that we are ourselves aware of the impossibility of perpetuating endless growth. Only then can we demand the correct action from our governments and authorities and only then can they respond suitably.

So we cannot wait for governments to realize or act on it. We have to actively, at a personal level, make the shift in paradigm and spread it from one person to the next, till there is a critical mass of belief that the government can be expected to act on.

- if we wait for the governments, it'll be too little, too late ;

- if we act as individuals, it'll be too little ;

- but if we act as **communities**, it might just be enough, just in time.

Yes, the response certainly has to be at a **community level** and based on a new collective belief.

For that, we need to holistically and systemically understand our predicament of energy shrinkage or we will only come up with responses such as "let us change our light bulbs to CFL" and "we must buy the latest energy efficient car". These, though necessary, are merely quantitative and not qualitative solutions and so do not make a systemic change.

We must remember that we are not talking about running the world the way it is. We are talking about reconceiving it first and then rebuilding a world that works on a completely different set of principles: steady-state instead of growth based; small and local instead of big and global; sharing instead of ceaseless competition; resilience instead of efficiency to increase compulsive productivity. And all this aims to ensure that we are in sync with the larger reality of energy decline.

This is not just a matter of upholding an ethically correct cultural ideology. It is simply about realizing what is going to be possible in a shrinking energy world. This also means shrinking of money.

Charles Eisenstein in his book *Sacred Economics: Money, Gift, and Society in the Age of Transition* explains that the habitual first response to an economic crisis is to hoard money – to accelerate the conversion of all kinds of Earth capital into money. We can see this happening with calls to drill for oil in Alaska, to commence deep-sea drilling, mine the bottom of the sea, tap the last strains of natural gas and so on.

Eisenstein explains how the creation of money in this manner has in fact impoverished us all. So, conversely, the destruction of money has the potential to enrich us. It offers the opportunity to reclaim parts of the lost commonwealth from the realm of money and property. We see this happening every time there is an economic recession, which I will illustrate at the end of this chapter with the example of Cuba. People can no longer pay for various goods and services, and so have to rely on friends and neighbours instead. This is a qualitative change. Where there is no money to facilitate transactions, gift economies re-emerge and new kinds of money are created. We forge new bonds and new relationships. And all these are out of the normal purview of quantitative economic growth.

This is going to happen anyway in the wake of economic shrinkage and the ensuing currency collapse, as people lose their jobs or become too poor to buy things. The only option then is to remove things from the realm of goods and services and return them to the realm of gifts, reciprocity, self-sufficiency and community sharing. People will help each other, and real communities will re-emerge. Even if you care mostly about the security of your own future, community is probably the best investment you can make. [13]

Let us now understand and structure this response through an approach called the Transition method.

The Transition Method

 **Transition**, as explained here, is a structured and conscious way of moving safely from our present high energy-consumption state based on fossil fuels, towards a low energy-consumption state of our solar energy budget as represented by the Third Curve.

The Transition concept emerged from work that permaculture designer Rob Hopkins had carried out with students of Kinsale Further Education College on an "Energy Descent Action Plan". It has now spread to over 840 initiatives in 35 countries around the globe.

The move to Transition begins when a small group comes together with a shared concern about shrinking supplies of cheap energy (peak oil), climate change and increasing economic downturn.

The concept that life post-oil might indeed be much more pleasant and fulfilling than today's lifestyle is at the heart of the Transition movement. This may seem be hard for certain people to visualize or accept but the movement explains that: "by shifting our mindset, we can actually recognize the coming post-cheap-oil era as an opportunity rather than a threat, and design the future low carbon age to be thriving, resilient and abundant – somewhere much better to live than our current alienated consumer culture based on greed, war and the myth of perpetual growth".

To prepare ourselves to accept this, we need to come to terms with the following:

- Infinite growth within a finite system (like planet Earth) is impossible.

- Energy decline is inevitable. We need to plan for it.

- Modern industrial society has lost the resilience to deal with energy shocks.

- Environmental collapse, climate change and peak oil are related and require that we start acting together now taking them all into account.

- If we plan and act early enough, and use our creativity and cooperation to unleash the genius within our local communities, we can build a future far more fulfilling and enriching, more connected to and more gentle on the Earth, than the life we have today.

We need to be careful that we don't confuse this with environmentalism because there is a crucial difference between plain environmentalism and the Transition approach.

Most people do not realize that environmentalism usually addresses individual behaviour and so gets trapped in individual issues such as reducing consumption or increasing efficiency or preserving the environment. Using CFL bulbs, sharing cars, saving our forests and rivers are useful but not enough. This is purely **quantity** related and has nothing to do with **quality**.

The Transition approach, in contrast, embodies both, the **quantitative** reduction of energy and consumption and a **qualitative** rebuilding of aspects of the world that have been lost. The Transition approach deals with the less obvious and tricky aspect of rebuilding the fabric of our world, which was destroyed by the wide-spread use of cheap energy.

In our pursuit for quantity, which is embodied by Perpetual Exponential Quantitative Growth, we completely lost track of something else called **"quality"** – an aspect of reality that is as real as quantity but hard to measure.

We usually think of quality in a quantitative measuring sense. We grade things as "high quality" or "low quality". But that is not the "quality" the Transition method is referring to. Quality here means the unique nature of something. 2 apples, or 2 trees or 2 people have different qualities in so many ways. If we did not measure or grade them one against the other, we would recognize the uniqueness of each. Each one is just what it is and that is an aspect of nature and reality beyond measurement. And measurement is a form of control.

No wonder our culture, which we call Civilization, is obsessed with control. Today's Civilization is built upon extensive measuring and quantifying, which are both essential to gaining control. But Civilization cannot get a grip around something like quality, because quality is beyond control. No wonder we come up with lines like "my daddy is the strongest" as a way of measuring love, or "my country is the best country" as a measure of national pride. We have forgotten that all daddies will be loved without measure and we all love the uniqueness of our place of birth with no aspersions on other places.

Therefore the Transition approach explains that we need to reconstruct a lot of the qualitative aspects of our world that the luxury of cheap oil and growth have wiped out: local economies, local networks, smaller grassroots enterprises, personal bonds, acts of caring and sharing, belief in personal skills and abilities, belief in quality over quantity and many more. None of these can be measured quantitatively. They are simply desirable qualities of a system. When we lose some or all of the above, we effectively lose a vital property of that system called **Resilience**.

Resilience is a qualitative aspect of natural systems like our environment and our social community and is therefore crucial to their survival. When a system is resilient it has the ability to maintain its capability to absorb change and external shocks. Therefore reviving resilience is the core guiding principle of the Transition approach that is taking root in countries all over the world in the wake of Peak Oil and the persisting economic collapse.

In order to rebuild a resilient post-oil economy, the Transition approach guides people to re-weave the web of our communities. This involves a revival of the qualitative aspects of our lives such as local relationships that were broken due to growth-based economics and rampant globalization. Individualism became the rule of the day so we forgot that we are part of a network that can only work collectively and not individually.

In response to this, the environmental movement is simply concerned with one question, "How can we keep everything going the way it is?" This amounts to simply feeding the **Concept Curve** with false solutions like solar, wind, nuclear and the whole gamut of oil-based pseudo alternatives. While conventional environmentalism is mainly giving out a message that says, "Why change ourselves if we can simply change our light bulbs?", this mainstream thought is nowhere near addressing a necessary qualitative change. No wonder the ordinary person feels extremely frustrated with the scope and effect of the environmental movement.

Learning to live within a realistic energy paradigm and its constraints implies letting go of many things, but most importantly, actively recovering the qualitative aspects of our community.

Efficiency vs. Resilience

The Modern Industrial World is based on maximizing economic growth by constantly increasing productivity and output while minimizing cost. This is what we call **efficiency**.

In attempting to achieve efficiency, our economic system has failed to value nature's redundancy, seeking to eliminate it instead. Ironically, it is the abundance of nature's redundancy itself that makes it work so effectively. By failing to respect natural redundancy and seeking to improve nature's efficiency and profitability in economic terms, the Modern Industrial World has mastered the technique of breaking natural systems apart and manipulating the pieces for short-term gain.

The history of our industrial civilization has therefore essentially been the story of gaining control over nature. Soil was tilled; rivers were dammed; the wild tamed into mono-agriculture; microorganisms trying to reclaim their food were wiped out by broadband chemicals; cattle-eating predators were hunted and eliminated; and pesticides, herbicides and antibiotics were liberally applied to crops to deal with those pesky insects. Little did we realize that the redundancy we eliminated in the name of efficiency limits our options for recovery.

So fittingly, we are facing the backlash of this control-based, profit maximizing, perpetual growth approach reflected in our ecological and subsequent financial collapse. We have to change our approach – resilience has to replace efficiency as an organizing principle of our economy. Efficiency makes the system dependent and vulnerable.

Still in the human-centric and growth-based world of today, our myths of performance, progress and development continue to reign. Our modern food system perfectly portrays how inflexible and frail a system and a society may become if it becomes so highly dependent on oil-based pesticides, farm machines and fertilizers that need cheap and regular oil supply for the production, shipping and processing of food.

RESILIENCE

Inversely, **resilience** is a concept that is based on the idea that a system, should be able to stomach a shock from the outside without coming apart. It has multiple paths for recovery and therefore the ability to adapt and change to its new circumstances with multiple options.

That is because nature is an interconnected web. It intrinsically relies on interdependence. Redundancy is innately built into nature and gives multiple paths to bounce out of failure.

The Transition approach understands that when you manipulate the individual pieces of a complex system, such as our community, our soils and our ecosystems, then you change that system in unintended ways that unknown to us make it vulnerable and prone to failure. We have ample evidence of this in the eco-collapse being experienced all around the world.

Another type of loss of resilience is seen in events such as a spate of power grid failures that have rippled across the U.S., empty super-market shelves in mega-cities like New York within 3 days of trucker strikes and piling of garbage beyond sanitary limits in France due to a garbage collectors strike. These are all examples of the loss of resilience in our industrialized, centralized world in the face of a single failure.

This is less likely to occur in India as in many less industrialized societies because resilience is intrinsic to our villages and small towns. Similar failures will have a lesser effect, except in cities that are based more on the centralized model. Yes, many things do need to change and improve in India but not at the expense of losing resilience.

The Transition approach helps us understand and address the importance of resilience and takes steps that allow us to nurture and rebuild it. And the core idea to achieving this is the idea of community.

Community Building

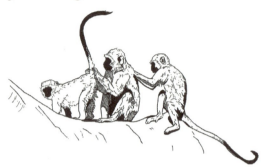

Before we discovered oil, our world depended on local networks of relationships and connections that we called our community.

Plentiful cheap oil made it possible for us to develop new long-distance, trade-based relationships. Therefore, our neighbours and local community were not so important to us as they did not contribute directly to our trade or business.

In short, we burnt our Social Capital – the bonds in family, community and society between people: love, respect, mutual caring, peace and harmony – for short-term monetary gain. This kind of capital may be invisible but it is the very basis of a community's health. These days we often live without meeting or knowing our neighbour. Life post-peak oil will require that we rebuild our community connections in order to increase its resilience.

However, achieving this requires more than mere **quantitative** reduction of consumption that is often emphasized by the environmental movement. We will have to relearn the old **qualitative** paradigm in the new context of energy shrinkage. No wonder there is a sense of powerlessness and isolation that the environmental approach can often generate, as was voiced by my guest at the lecture. No wonder she felt that she could not generate action, either as an individual or as a community.

This is countered in the Transition approach, because its first goal is to rely on a small group coming together spontaneously to discuss and digest how the impending energy decline and economic downturn will adversely affect their lives and community. Each person can feel that they are not alone in their awareness of the predicaments of Peak Oil and End of Growth, giving each individual and the community a sense of empowerment as people feel part of something larger than themselves.

To organize these groups, the Transition approach takes some valuable lessons from the nature model which is self-organizing. There is no central control. This makes the replication of smaller units of action in communities easier and more vibrant.

Moving from Global back to Local

Focusing on the development of our community intrinsically involves the move back from global to local. Before cheap oil became a rule of thumb, creating the short span illusion of a globalized world, our planet had always been local. Energy decline will inevitably eliminate globalization as an option. In retrospect, the Oil Age will be seen as a span of 150 years which allowed man to move away from a primarily local lifestyle only to come back to it again on the down side of Hubbert's curve.

The illusion created in our mind today is that global is a step forward and ensures a better life. But leading a life with less energy and a more local and resilient focus can also lead us towards a better quality of life in the future. A solidified and lively local economy would have many perks compared to what is happening today in our global economy. Moving towards a local economy in the face of energy shrinkage has become scary to us because we have always valued growth and have labelled our expanding global economy as development and progress. Anything that goes in the opposite direction of that trend is considered as outright collapse and failure.

Yet, if we consider the Transition Approach to address key aspects to our survival like food, agriculture, local materials and local products, we realize that in fact the opposite is true – the future promises to be more secure and lasting.

Local Food

Food is certainly the most vital part of our lives. Consequently, food must be local for our community's safety and well-being.

Contrary to the idea above, our energy-intensive modern food system has become extremely complex, leaving behind a record rate of environmental damage, energy dilapidation and social inequity.

The food situation in India is an emerging tragedy. Being the second most populated country in the world, India is rapidly losing its agrarian nature by chasing the global model of long-distance food. This energy intensive and market-based system ends up creating the illusion of shortage when in fact we have enough to feed all.

India, which was fundamentally local in its food requirement, is hastily changing its pattern to grow and ship food for market gain under the illusion that doing so spells progress. From a purely economic point of view, it made sense to chase that greater margin of profit by making food non-local. But of course this was only made possible by cheap fossil fuel energy. All this is soon to be trumped by high energy prices.

The Transition approach stresses the importance of local food because it makes sense in so many ways.

- **Eating local benefits the local economy.** Would you rather help your neighbourhood grocer subsist or a huge supermarket chain you have no relationship with?

- **Eating local is more environmentally friendly.** Food that travels long distances requires means of transportation that run on fossil fuels, creating pollution and global warming.

- **Locally grown fruits and vegetables are more fresh, nutritious and taste much better.** Check it out for yourself by tasting some countryside grown food. Besides, they don't cause cancer or other illnesses.

- **Buying local food keeps us in touch with the seasons.** By following the Earth's seasons, we eat foods when they have reached their best taste and nutritional value, are the most abundant and are cheaper. Also there is a feeling of uniqueness related to a certain time of the year. The sound of the *koyal* bird in summer connects with the sultry heat building up that finally translates into the joy of eating mangoes. And that too not all the varieties at one go. First the *hafoos*, then *langda*, then *chausa* then *daseri* and so on as the season progresses. This lends a variation to the year and preserves our cyclic feeling of time.

The other lethal trend is that food has become a commodity to be traded and speculated upon. This has resulted in high and volatile prices for even basic food items. So in fact, rather than serving a fundamental purpose of survival, the commodification of food is catering to the concept of speculation to propagate growth of money.

Alternative Agriculture

Modern agriculture is the de facto method practiced around the world. But time has shown how this method is a chemical and aggressively organized assault on our soil to maximize its productivity rate as if it were a factory. All this was made possible by cheap oil.

Cheap oil has corrupted our view of how food should be produced, resulting in aggressive tillage, the use of toxic pesticides and fertilizers produced with natural gas and oil, plus extensive irrigation. These toxic and energy intensive practices have destroyed the soil's health and we celebrated this as the Green Revolution.

The sole effect of this green revolution was nothing more than to transform our soil from what was a living colony that worked as a complex web, into a sponge that holds water and needs to be fed with artificial nutrients in the form of fertilizers.

Sadly and dangerously, the obvious failure of chemical farming is being complemented with solutions like genetically modified seeds and foods, presented as the next level of attaining food security. I leave it to the author of another book to dismantle the illusion behind this new madness of GM food and the assault on the fabric of life at the very genetic level.

Here, I restrict my argument by saying that no serious transition can be made without completely re-examining the way we grow our food. It is not just a question of not putting chemicals and calling it organic. It is a matter of learning how to keep the vitality of the soil intact and working with nature rather than against it.

For a start, we are facing the enormous responsibility and work of rebuilding our soil's fertility and replenishing it with the nutrients necessary for wholesome food production. There are many disciplines that address this: permaculture, bio-dynamic farming, natural farming and others.

Permaculture, for instance, is a methodology for designing sustainable human habitats and modelling them after natural ecosystems. The permaculture model emphasizes a move away from industrial agriculture towards a small-scale, diversified, and localized system of food production.

David Holmgren, one of the originators of the concept, defines permaculture as:

> "Consciously designed landscapes which mimic the patterns and relationships found in nature, while yielding an abundance of food, fibre and energy for provision of local needs. People, their buildings and the ways in which they organize themselves are central to permaculture. Thus the permaculture vision of permanent or sustainable agriculture has evolved to one of permanent or sustainable culture". [14]

It makes sense therefore that alternative agriculture models, like permaculture design, should underpin the thinking and planning behind any Transition project.

Local Materials & Products

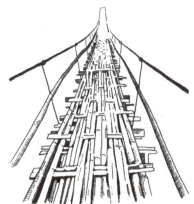

Supporting local materials and products is crucial to developing community resilience.

Transporting materials and products to distant markets consumes a lot of energy and is costly because it requires the shipping, processing and packaging of goods. It also entails a lot of pollution. When we buy products coming in from long distances, local money is funnelled out towards distant trading centers, which makes a community more economically vulnerable.

Purchasing local products generates local jobs, as well as encourages local business owners to contribute to the community by supporting local initiatives and organizations that empowers the community by making it self-reliant and therefore more resilient to transient changes in the world around.

Peak Oil Awareness

Above all, in order to prepare for Transition, we need a huge amount of deprogramming from the industrial mindset. We have to engage every level of the community in the core understanding of Peak Oil and its ultimate impact on society, leading to an inversion of rules of classical economics which means an inversion of Growth to Shrinkage.

I find it bewildering that while our education system makes us aware of principles, ranging from the laws of gravity to quantum physics, it ignores the most basic aspect of reality – that the Earth gives us resources in a bell curve and that perpetual exponential growth is a dangerous illusion.

We therefore have to slowly work on the painful task of bringing Peak Oil awareness into a wider and wider circle of people to expand the new collective belief.

We have to engage school teachers and college professors in Peak Oil discussions and Transition group activities so that they can understand it first and then divert their expertise towards making the next generation aware of it as part of the regular curriculum.

We have to engage the business and banking community to make them understand the new paradigm of shrinkage. This will lead them to interpret the current difficulties they are facing to achieve growth as a new and normal macro phenomenon and therefore will help them make realistic plans for the future of their businesses.

This will then widen to engaging local officials in the activities of the Transition group so that they are open to accepting new policies that encourage Transition group efforts, like local food initiatives and community building activities. Making "peak" an acceptable four letter word is only possible through a community level acceptance of its reality.

Since I became aware of Peak Oil, I have noticed that at first it was simply ignored and then mocked. But after the 2008 economic collapse, it has started appearing in media enclosed in quotes like "peak oil" to suggest that it is not really a truth but a speculation. We have to overcome this denial and urgently start incorporating Peak Oil reality into our education, policies and development plans. Being coy or evasive about it is not going to change the geology of this planet.

India is yet blissfully unaware of Peak Oil. It is imperative that India wake up to the concept and the reality of Peak Oil. Being a country with over 1.2 billion people, with a small land mass, a high growth rate and no significant oil reserves, we are sleepwalking into disaster.

Cuba – A Real Peak Oil Story

I end this book with the example of Cuba – the only country in the world that has faced the most extreme version of Peak Oil. Their successful response is exemplary. It is imperative we learn from it and take heart that there is indeed a valid response to the inevitable energy descent.

With the fall of the Soviet Union in 1990, Cuba registered an overnight decline of oil imports. As a result Cuba's economy took a direct plunge. Cubans were confronted with living a situation comparable to that of a sudden and extreme onset of Peak Oil and that Cubans refer to as "The Special Period". Oil imports fell by 75% and food by 80% resulting in transport services crumbling down and food and fuel becoming rationed. The average Cuban lost almost 10 kg in four years. Blackouts and water shortage became a Cuban's daily bread and the Cuban currency devalued to the point of being useless. Despite all of this, the country survived and the resilience of Cuban communities prospered. The Cuban example is therefore an excellent observation ground for understanding how to deal with Peak Oil and Economic Collapse.

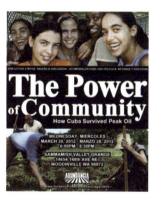

A documentary called **The Power of Community** directed by Faith Morgan and released in 2006, explores how Cubans dealt with their own economic and energy crisis, developing a local system that very much resembles that of the Transition approach described in earlier sections.

Morgan was amazed by the resilience of Cubans and realized that the country's economic impasse was not solved by finding new energy sources, but by shifting the people's economic mindset and tackling their situation with a community approach.

She learned how Cubans transitioned from an industrial agricultural system similar to ours to organic farming and local food markets. Cuba went from using 21,000 tons of pesticide in the '80s to a mere 1,000 tons in 2005.

Following the economic collapse, Cubans from all walks of life started exploring the benefits of more traditional or alternative farming methods such as composting, permaculture, vermiculture and crop rotation. People got together to find and make the most out of any urban or rural area that would be available to grow food. Today 80% of Cuba's food production is organic. This has not only improved the soil's quality but also the general health of the people.

Fuel scarcity and the resulting failure and unreliability of the public transportation system prompted the government to provide over a million bicycles to a population who adopted cycling as a practice in their daily lives. This also entailed an improvement in general public health.

It was clear that there was something intrinsic to Cuban people that facilitated this transition, and that was the sense of community. The cooperative nature of the response effectively proved that all this did not need high-tech solutions but relationships between people. This was community and resilience building at its raw best.

The Cuban approach intuitively embodied all the principles of the Transition approach – rebuilding the soil, rebuilding the community and its resilience, growing local food, developing alternative and earth-friendly agriculture and encouraging local initiative. All this was lost because of plentiful cheap oil.

The Cuba experience therefore is a showcase for the rest of the world to learn the core principles of Transition in dealing with energy descent. Though the conditions in each area and country will be different, the core principles remain the same. The cultural perspective of revitalizing the local community has to take center stage in all our plans to cope with energy descent. This is a qualitative change and the only kind that can actually make the necessary quantitative change of consumption that is also necessary.

If Cuba could do it, so can any part of the world, provided we first recognize the new reality of shrinking energy and money and then adopt the principles of the Transition method.

This book urges that it is imperative we globally act now and start preparing for our inevitable but meaningful journey down Hubbert's curve to the eternal Third Curve.

Sources & References

MURPHY, DAVID. *theoildrum.com*

HEWITT, MIKE. *DollarDaze.com*

ASPO Newsletter #100

SCHUMACHER, EF. *Small is Beautiful: Economics as if People Mattered.* Harper Perennial. 2010.

BLACK-SCHOLES. Wikipedia. *en.wikipedia.org/wiki/Black–Scholes*

BROWN, ELLEN. Global Research. *It's the Derivatives, Stupid! Why Fannie, Freddie, AIG had to be Bailed Out.* 2008. (Robert Chapman original quote from James Wesley, "Derivatives – The Mystery Man Who'll Break the Global Bank at Monte Carlo," SurvivalBlog.com (September 2006).

STEWART, IAN. *Guardian News and Media Ltd.* "The mathematical equation that caused the banks to crash". 2012.

BOULDING, KENNETH E. United States Congress. *Energy reorganization act of 1973: Hearings, 93rd Congress, 1st session.* 1973.

Reed Business Information. *The Disease and the Trigger.* Tribune Media Services. 2008.

ABBEY, EDWARD. *The Journey Home: Some Words in Defense of the American West.* Plume. 1991.

Center for Sustainable Systems Newsletter : US Food System Factsheets

ZABEL, GRAHAM. *Peak People: The Interrelationship between Population Growth and Energy Resources,* London School of Economics, MSc Demography/Energy, Economics, originally published by Energy Bulletin. 2009.

Ranken Energy, *http://www.ranken-energy.com/Products%20from%20 Petroleum.htm*

DEFFEYES, KENNETH. *Hubbert's Peak: The Impending World Oil Shortage.* Princeton University Press. 2001.

MARTENSON, CHRIS. *The Crash Course.* 2009.

GHANTA, PRAVEEN. *Truecostblog.com.* http://truecostblog. com/2012/01/21/countries-by-peak-oil-date-2011-data-update/

CAMPBELL, COLIN J. SunWorld. 1995.

CHEFURKA, PAUL. Paulchefurka.ca

RUBIN, JEFF & BUCHANAN, PETER. *"What's the Real Cause of the Global Recession?"* StrategEcon, CIBC World Markets Inc. and Bloomberg. 2008.

HIRSCH, ROBERT L. *Hirsch Report.* U.S. Dept. of Energy. 2005.

U.S. Military. *Joint Operating Environment Report.* 2010.

WHEATCROFT, PATIENCE. *"The Next Crisis: Prepare for Peak Oil".* The Wall Street Journal. 2010.

DONNELLY, JOHN. *"Price rise and new deep-water technology opened up offshore drilling"* The Boston Globe. 2005.

GREER, JOHN MICHAEL. *The Archdruid Report.* thearchdruidreport. blogspot.com/

BARTLETT, ALBERT. *Arithmetic, Population and Energy.* University of Colorado at Boulder. 2011.

TVERBERG, GAIL. *World Energy Consumption by Source,* Based on Vaclav Smil estimates from Energy Transitions: History, Requirements and Prospects together with BP Statistical Data for 1965 and subsequent. ourfiniteworld.com.

VAN DER VEER, JEROEN. *"Three Hard Truths about the World's Energy Crisis".* The Standard. 2007.

BP Statistical Review of World Energy 2012

GOODMAN, JAMES. Ilovemountains.org

STOCKMAN, VIVIAN. Ohvec.org. Flyover courtesy Southwings.org.

STRAHAN, DAVID. *The Last Oil Shock: A Survival Guide to the Imminent Extinction of Petroleum Man.* John Murray. 2008.

BAINES, COLIN. The Co-operative Group

SIMMONS, MATTHEW R. *Twilight in the Desert: The Coming Saudi Oil Shock and the World Economy.* John Wiley & Sons. 2006.

U.S. National Archives images.

ROY, ARUNDHATI. *The Greater Common Good.* India Book Distributor (Bombay) Ltd. 1999.

Transition Network logo. Transition Network.org

HOLMGREN, DAVID. *The Essence of Permaculture.* Holmgren Design Services. 2006.

MORGAN, FAITH. *Power of Community.* Community Service, Inc. 2009.

Bibliography

1. HIRSCH, R. L. "Robert Hirsch on Peak Oil Mitigation". *Global Public Media.* 17 Nov. 2005 http://old.globalpublicmedia.com/robert_hirsch_on_peak_oil_mitigation.
2. WHEATCROFT, PATIENCE. "The Next Crisis: Prepare for Peak Oil". *The Wall Street Journal.* February 11, 2010.
3. DONNELLY, JOHN. "Price rise and new deep-water technology opened up offshore drilling" *The Boston Globe.* 11 December 2005. 21 August 2008.
4. "The Truth about Gas Drilling and your Health: Health Risks from the Fracking of Gas Wells". *Catskill Mountainkeeper.* http://www.catskillmountainkeeper.org/sample-page/the-truth-about-gas-drilling-and-your-health/.
5. Peak Oil – Unconventional Sources – Wikipedia. http://en.wikipedia.org/wiki/Peak_oil#Peak_oil_for_individual_nations.
6. ANDREWS, JAMES M. "The Biofuels Scam". *American Thinker.* 07 Nov 2010. http://www.americanthinker.com/2010/11/the_biofuels_scam.html.
7. Greenpeace Canada, Questions and Answers about the Alberta Tar Sands. http://www.greenpeace.org/canada/en/recent/tarsandsfaq/
8. "H2Oil Factsheet: The Tailing Ponds". *H2Oil website.* Retrieved 29 March 2013. http://h2oildoc.com/home/tar_sands.
9. http://dirtyoilsands.org/tarsands.
10. PAIMPILLIL, JOSEPH SEBASTIAN. *Reservoir de-siltation and its impacts on wetland water quality – A Case Study.* Center for Earth Research and Environment Management. www.gwsp.org/fileadmin/GCI_conference/Products/Pos_pres_-_Paimpillil_-_Reservoir_de-siltation.pdf.

11. Nuclear Power in the United States. Wikipedia. http://en.wikipedia. org/wiki/Nuclear_power_in_the_United_States.

12. FLEMING, DAVID. *The Lean Guide to Nuclear Energy.* Nov 2007. www. theleaneconomyconnection.net/nuclear/index.html.

13. EISENSTEIN, CHARLES. *Sacred Economics: Money, Gift, and Society in the Age of Transition.* Random House Inc Clients Kindle Edition. 2011.

14. HOLMGREN, DAVID. *The Essence of Permaculture.* Holmgren Design Services. 2006.

Reading & Reference Material

1. Fundamental Reading

Books:

- *The Party's Over* by Richard Heinberg
- *Powerdown* by Richard Heinberg
- *Snake Oil: How Fracking's False Promise of Plenty Imperils Our Future* by Richard Heinberg
- *Twilight in the Desert* by Matthew Simmons
- *The Long Descent: A User's Guide to the End of the Industrial Age* by John Michael Greer
- *The Long Emergency* by James Howard Kunstler
- *Regaining Paradise - towards a fossil fuel free society* by T. Vijayendra
- *The Collapse of Complex Societies* by Joseph A. Tainter.
- *Out of Gas* by David Goodstein
- *Overshoot* by William Catton
- *The Age of Oil is Over* by Matthew Savinar
- *The Final Energy Crisis* edited by Andrew McKillop
- *High Noon for Natural Gas* by Julian Darley
- *The End of Oil : On the Edge of a Perilous New World* by Paul Roberts

Prominent Peak Oil Speakers:

RICHARD HEINBERG: I would begin with books by Richard Heinberg, such as *The Party's Over, Powerdown, Oil Depletion Protocol* and *Searching for a Miracle*. Heinberg is level-headed, impartial and treats the matter with due diligence, giving a genuinely good look at the various paths we could take, while considering all the practical limits as well as the possibilities for innovation. Anyone wishing to begin understanding the subject should consult his books.

KENNETH S. DEFFEYES: I recommend *Hubbert's Peak: The Impending*

World Oil Shortage and Beyond Oil: The View from Hubbert's Peak.

JOHN MICHAEL GREER: A very balanced, enlightened, elegantly worded and consistent view of energy depletion. I would suggest reading Greer's *The Long Descent* and *The Ecotechnic Future.* They are handbooks for understanding the issue from a practical perspective. Highly recommended. His weekly blog, *The Archdruid Report* is a must read for me. Visit it at thearchdruidreport.blogspot.in/

GAIL TVERBERG: *Introduction to Peak Oil* is a clearly written introduction to the science of peak oil, building up from the basics. The link is www.darkoptimism.org/PeakOilIntro.pdf

PROFESSOR ALBERT A. BARTLETT (Professor Emeritus in Nuclear Physics at University of Colorado at Boulder): For a complete reference on Exponential Growth, read his lectures at his website www.albartlett.org/

MATT SIMMONS: Matt Simmons, long time energy analyst who studied energy for 34 years, effectively confronts the complacent belief that there are ample oil reserves in Saudi Arabia in his book *Twilight in the Desert* and has created a compelling case that Saudi Arabia production will soon reach a peak, after which its production will decline and the world will be confronted with a catastrophic oil shortage.

2. FILMS, DOCUMENTARIES & INTERVIEWS ON PEAK OIL:

The End of Suburbia and *A Crude Awakening* are two excellent peak oil documentaries that are purchasable on DVD.

CHRIS MARTENSON: To understand the connection between Peak Oil and the Credit Crisis you have to take a look at videos at: www.chrismartenson.com

RICHARD HEINBERG on One World TV (video) is a 7 minute interview extract in which Heinberg outlines the basics of Peak Oil. It may be watched at http://youtu.be/DHXdS9XYVs8 If you want a little more of the detail behind this, read his article *The View from Oil's Peak* at http://richardheinberg.com/184-the-view-from-oil%E2%80%99s-peak. Heinberg also appeared on Radio 4 in September 2008, the audio from which is available at, www.darkoptimism.org/2008/09/27/bbc-radio-4-discuss-peak-oil-intelligently/#post-98

DR. COLIN CAMPBELL is a retired British petroleum geologist who predicted that oil production would peak by 2007. He has given excellent lectures and presentations which may be found on Youtube.

PEAK OIL FILMS: Links to various Peak Oil films, documentaries and features available online can be found at http://www.dynamiclist. com/?node=c47dd8da-68dd-4db4-8307-efed06a61aef.

PEAK OIL? : This is a 44 minute TV special from Four Corners (Australia), viewable online at abc.net.au/4corners/special_eds/20060710/

Interviews with key Peak Oil Speakers: These are available at http:// youtu.be/UUmwyoVTnqM

3. ADDITIONAL READING MATERIAL ON PEAK OIL

THE OIL DRUM: This website publishes carefully thought-out articles discussing energy and our future in a serious manner. It attracts many of the best-informed observers. Link at www.theoildrum.com/

DAVID STRAHAN: Strahan is a journalist and documentary film-maker, and his book *The Last Oil Shock* – focusing on the UK – is by far the most readable guide to our Peak Oil predicament. Thoroughly recommended reading for beginners and Peak Oil experts alike. Link at www.lastoilshock.com/

ENERGY BULLETIN: An outstanding clearinghouse for current information news and events regarding the peak in global energy supply, climate change and related topics. Link at energybulletin.net/

THE POST CARBON INSTITUTE: The Post Carbon Institute carries most of the significant books on the issue. It is a storehouse of detailed technical information on Peak Oil and Energy Depletion. Link at www.postcarbon. org/publications/book-list/

ASPO - The Association for the Study of Peak Oil and Gas: Another balanced and technical site for collecting critical information and data on Peak Oil and Energy Depletion. Excellent articles here to explain to the common person too. Link at www.peakoil.net/

WOLF AT THE DOOR: A beginner's guide to Peak oil. Their link is http:// wolf.readinglitho.co.uk/

OIL AND FOOD PRODUCTION: Essays *The Oil We Eat* by Richard Manning and "Eating Fossil Fuels" by Dale Allen Pfeiffer both look at modern agricultures' dependence on fossil fuels. Both are highly recommended.

DIE-OFF: The title sounds Malthusian but the book is an excellent and scholarly archive of research. The original peak oil website is at http://www.dieoff.com/

PEAK OIL BLUES: This excellent and friendly site is run by professionally trained psychotherapists to help those trying to come to terms with Peak Oil and its impact on their life and plans. Link at www.peakoilblues.com/

4. US & OTHER GOVERNMENT REPORTS ON PEAK OIL

THE HIRSCH REPORT: The 2005 report commissioned by the U.S. Department of Energy (full title: *Peaking of World Oil Production: Impacts, Mitigation, and Risk Management*) concludes that "the peaking of world oil production presents the U.S. and the world with an unprecedented risk management problem"; that without timely mitigation the economic, social and political impacts will be abrupt, revolutionary and permanent; and that mitigation "must be initiated more than a decade in advance of peaking". Link at www.theleaneconomyconnection.net/HirschReport.pdf

THE ALL PARTY PARLIAMENTARY GROUP ON PEAK OIL AND GAS: This group, founded in June 2007, is made up of MPs and Lords from the UK Government. They are discussing and investigating the debate regarding the date of global peak oil production and looking at the range of possible impacts, mitigations and solutions. Link at www.appgopo.org.uk/

THE SECOND REPORT OF THE UK INDUSTRY TASKFORCE ON PEAK OIL AND ENERGY SECURITY (ITPOES): A group of leading business people today call for urgent action to prepare the UK for Peak Oil. The report finds that oil shortages, insecurity of supply and price volatility will destabilize economic, political and social activity potentially by 2015. You can download it from peakoiltaskforce.net/wp-content/uploads/2010/02/final-report-uk-itpoes_report_the-oil-crunch_feb2010i.pdf. The 2010 Oil Crunch report is available to download peakoiltaskforce.net/download-the-report/2010-peak-oil-report/. The 2008 report can be downloaded at peakoiltaskforce.net/wp-content/uploads/2008/10/oil-report-final.pdf.

AUSTRALIAN GOVERNMENT REPORT ON PEAK OIL: The Australian Daily Telegraph published today a story on a leaked government report (BITRE 117) which (optimistically) calculated peak oil around 2017, followed by permanent decline. The report can be downloaded here: ianmcpherson.com/blog/audio/Australian_Govt_Oil_supply_trends.pdf

New Zealand Government Report Warns Peak Oil is Imminent: The report discusses it but refuses to use the word Peak Oil because that admits the one way decline of oil. This makes it just sound like a temporary constraint that can be dealt with by more investment, etc. Anyway, read it at www.permaculture.org.au/files/nz_peak_oil_study.pdf

5. Books on Transition, Permaculture, Natural Farming & Alternative Economics

One Straw Revolution by MASANOBU FUKUOKA. The all-time classic elegantly contests classical views on nature and life itself, countering them with a humbling approach that helps the reader understand simple and intelligent ways to relate to our environment and our community.

The Sharing Solution: How to Save Money, Simplify Life and Build Community by JANELLE ORSI & EMILY DOSKOW. This practical guide to community sharing provides sustainable answers to a forthcoming lack of energy and resources. The book brings together the environmental and social benefits of sharing locally and globally.

Small is Beautiful: Economics as if People Mattered by E. F. SCHUMACHER. A classic that first reversed the Western world's view on economics. This is a must read for anyone beginning the journey of transition from the world of Big to the world that will be possible beyond oil.

The Transition Handbook: From Oil Dependency to Local Resilience by ROB HOPKINS. Hopkins, a teacher of permaculture and natural building and a cofounder of the Transition Network, writes a practical guide and urges a community response – local sustainability made fun – in which groups grapple with issues like food, transportation, energy, building materials, and waste and even develop their own local currency. Hopkins takes our "addiction" to oil literally, and so we will read of "post-petroleum stress disorder", and see applied addictions psychology helping to ease the townies' withdrawal symptoms.

Permaculture: Principles and Pathways beyond Sustainability by DAVID HOLMGREN. Holmgren draws a correlation between every aspect of how we organize our lives, communities and landscapes and our ability to creatively adapt to the ecological realities that shape human destiny.